Running You

PLAYGROUP OR NURSERY

Running Your Own

PLAYGROUP OR NURSERY

Jenny Willison

KOGAN PAGE

Acknowledgements

I should like to thank the PPA for permission to reproduce its Tenancy Agreement and Contracts of Employment and for its help. I should also like to thank all the organisations mentioned in the book which have supplied up-to-date information. Many thanks to the proprietors and staff from playgroups, nursery schools and other privately funded facilities whom I interviewed and to the Apples Nursery School for permission to reproduce their publicity leaflet.

First published in Great Britain in 1989 by
Kogan Page Limited, 120 Pentonville Road,
London N1 9JN

British Library Cataloguing in Publication Data
Willison, Jenny
Running your own playgroup or nursery. - (Kogan Page working for yourself series)
1. Great Britain. Playgroups. Organisation
I. Title
372'.216

ISBN 1-85091-669-1

Typeset by DP Photosetting, Aylesbury, Bucks
Printed and bound in Great Britain by
Biddles Limited, Guildford

Contents

Acknowledgements 4

1. **Introduction** 9

2. **Playground or Nursery?** 11
What form of child care? 11; Definitions 12; Part-time or full-time care and how many children? 17

3. **Finance and Premises** 18
A scheme of things to do 18; Finance 18; Agencies offering advice 23; Premises: layout of playgroup or nursery 23; Business identity 25; Registration 26; A name 26; Fire regulations 27; Number of children to one loo 27; Building conversion and planning permission 27; Outdoor facilities 27; Buying a playgroup or nursery 28

4. **Getting and Keeping Helpers** 29
Child to helper ratio 29; Child care qualifications 29; Selection 33; Job description 35; Letter offering employment 37; Contract or letter of employment 38; Registration of helpers 38; Dismissal 39; Legislation 39; Supervision 42; Daily duties 42; Salaries 42

5. **Promotion and Advertising** 45
Letterheads and business stationery 45; Press release 46; Local press 47; Leaflets and brochures 48; Local authority lists 50; Yellow Pages 50; Independent Schools Information Service (ISIS) 51; Registration form 51; Advertising 51; Recommendations 53; Open days, fêtes and bazaars 53

6. **Equipment and Administration** 55
Equipment 55; How to set up for £500 62; Administration 63; Cooking, food and drink 64; Free milk 65; Fund raising 66

7. **Insurance** 68
Types of insurance 68; How to make a claim

74; Inventory of equipment 75; Child care associations 76

8. Health and Safety **80**
Immunisation 80; Quick guide to infectious diseases 81; Reaction to milk, eggs, wheat or fish 82; Allergies 82; Balanced diet 82; Food storage and cooking 83; Food additives and E numbers 83; Windows 84; Doors 84; Electricity supply 85; Gas supply 85; Cot safety 85; Stairs 86; Fire prevention 86; Road safety 86; First aid box 86; First aid courses 87; Keep them safe 87; Other accidents 88; Accident book and reporting accidents to your local authority 89; Suspected child abuse 89; HIV-positive children or not? 89

9. Lessons or Play? **91**
Drawing and painting 92; Printing 92 Composite pictures 93; Making toys, puppets and mobiles 93; Playdough, plasticine and clay 93; Cooking 93; Playhouse and imaginary play 93; Sewing and threading 94; Singing and making music 94; Jigsaw puzzles, picture lotto and dominoes 94; Weighing and measuring 94; Eating together 95; Outdoor activities 95; Games 95; Books 95; Telling the time 96; Colours, numbers and letters 96; Memory and odd one out 96; Science 97; Maps and different ethnic groups 97; Computers 97; Learning to read and write 97

10. Accounts **99**
Receipts and payments 99; Stationery for keeping accounts 101; Bank account 102; Doing the books 103; Petty cash 104; Cash book 109; Preparing annual accounts 111; Your bank statement 115; Sending out the term's accounts 117; Paying invoices 119; Salaries 119; Registration with the Collector of Taxes 123; Form P45 or P46 123; PAYE and National Insurance contributions 124; Hourly payment and overtime 125; Deducting National Insurance contributions 125; Deducting PAYE 126; Wages slips 127; Deductions working sheet P11 128; End of year return 128; Computerisation 129; The Collector of Taxes PAYE audit 129

11. **Childminding** 131
Registration 132; Insurance 133; Lunches and other meals 133; Agreement between parent and childminder 133; Child's record card 135; Registration of child with the Social Services Department of your local authority 135; Rates 135; Keeping simple accounts 135; Competition 138; Prospects and support 138

12. **Courses** 140
National Nursery Examination Board Certificate course 141; Scottish Nursery Nurses' Board registration 142; Scottish Vocational Education Council 143; The Business and Technician Education Council National Diploma in Caring Services (Nursery Nursing) 143; State-funded nursery nurses college of further education courses 144; Independent nursery training college courses 144; Pre-school Playgroups Association courses 146; London Montessori Centre courses 146; Montessori workshops 147; St Nicholas Montessori College courses 147; Registered General Nurse and Registered Sick Children's Nurse 148; Certificate of Education in Nursery Teaching and Certificate of Education in Infant Teaching 148; Correspondence courses 148; Open University courses 148; Business courses 148

13. **'How I Started'** 150

14. **Addresses** 158

15. **Further Reading** 170

Index 171

Chapter 1
Introduction

There has never been a better time for setting up privately funded playgroups and nurseries. In this book all types of privately funded pre-school child care facilities are discussed.

Those setting up and running voluntary groups in the community or groups funded by statutory bodies will also find this book useful. Some voluntary groups registered as charities are able to obtain grants to boost their funds. The Pre-school Playgroups Association (PPA) has an extensive publications list that will be of use to them. A privately funded group differs from these groups in one respect only. The privately funded child care facility aims to make a profit or at least to provide the proprietors with a reasonable income. Other groups in the community do not. Since raising children is very worthwhile and, as a child's character is malleable up to the age of seven, it is important that all groups offer a good standard of pre-school education, play and care to mothers who need it. This book looks at these subjects in detail.

In many regions private nurseries form the single largest provision outside local authority nursery schools and classes. Many bodies, and individuals, oppose the idea of four-year-olds in infant classes, so the private sector could provide even more places for under-fives.

As nursery education is not a statutory provision, some London boroughs and county councils may reduce the level of nursery education. Others may increase their facilities for the under-fives. In fact, more nursery schools are being built. Any losses could be combatted by the introduction of more child care groups in the private sector.

The problem of child care is less acute for those mothers who have decided to give up full-time employment during their family's pre-school years, but they are increasingly demanding some form of child care. To set up and run a playgroup or nursery school for children from this group of mothers, in which children stay for only part of the day, is a much less daunting task than establishing a creche, day nursery or workplace nursery.

More companies nowadays are receptive to the idea of

workplace nurseries. A creche is planned for the BBC at White City, London, and a child care voucher scheme (derived from the luncheon voucher scheme) has been introduced by Blue Arrow Personnel Services. Many employers now offer a subsidy towards child care for their employees who have young children as a means of attracting staff.

In this book topics such as registration of playgroups and nurseries with the Social Services Department of a local authority, funding the venture, finding suitable premises, getting and keeping the right staff, insurance, promotion, keeping accounts, equipping the premises, and the day-to-day running of a playgroup or nursery are described in some detail. The different types of group are defined in Chapter 2.

As this is an industry run by women, the playgroup or nursery owners and helpers are referred to as 'she'. Some men are good with children and they should be encouraged to take up this business if they wish. But they may well find that they are more suited to financing the venture and keeping accounts, and to employing helpers to work with the children. This may sound like a reinforcement of the male and female roles, but, even in these days of more equality between the sexes, it is still women who bear most of the responsibility (and the cost) of child care.

'Helper' is used throughout the book to describe a person paid to work in a child care facility. This is not to demean the status of the often well-qualified child care workforce but is used for convenience only. Nursery nurses, teachers, playgroup leaders, Montessori teachers, nannies, even parents, and many more are included in this group.

Organisations mentioned in this book are listed alphabetically in Chapter 14, unless they are publishers (the bookseller will order for you) or are likely to be in your local phone book. Since most child care organisations are non-profit making enclose a stamped and self-addressed envelope when writing for information. All prices were correct at the time of going to press, but it is advisable to check them in case changes have occurred in the meantime.

Much of the information has been obtained from child care organisations, talking to people, reading the press and my own personal experiences working with the founder members and playgroup leaders at St Luke's Playgroup, London.

Chapter 2

Playgroup or Nursery?

Parents who work, have other family commitments such as a new baby or an elderly relative, want to study, want free time to go to the hairdressers, go shopping or go to the dentist, etc, or live in small flats and do not wish babysitters or nannies to visit their homes, may require paid help during their child's pre-school years.

The child care services available to those families are defined below for clarity. Others might define the facilities differently. The many terms used in this field and the variation in child to helper ratios across the country make it confusing.

The aim of a privately funded group is to offer a good facility and to make a profit or at least to provide the proprietors with a reasonable income. During the early years the proprietors might choose to plough back any profits into the business. For example, getting the necessary equipment can be costly. However, if the business fails or has to be sold, the equipment belongs to the proprietors and can be sold off with the business.

Anybody wishing to set up a privately funded child care facility must follow the legal procedure which includes registering with the Social Services Department of the local authority. Reading through the following definitions might help you to decide on the kind of facility you wish to set up.

What form of child care?

The age of the cared-for child will often dictate the type of child care facility needed by a family. A family may use several forms of child care as its child grows older, for example childminder, childminder and playgroup, full-time nursery school and then infants' school.

Young babies can be looked after by a childminder. Childminding rates are comparatively inexpensive, the hours are flexible, and the child can go to the minder's home for more than 40 weeks a year if necessary. The childminder is self-employed. She is running a business and hopes to make a profit. A large income cannot be generated, since there always has to be a ratio of one minder to three children, or less if her own children are pre-school age. However, the minder can make some money for herself, does not have to go out of the home to work, can look after her own children at the same time, and be at home after school with any older children. Chapter 11 gives a comprehensive account of childminding.

A pre-school child or baby could go to a creche, day nursery or workplace nursery. Rates vary but they are usually high because this facility is labour intensive, requires extra space and takes children for the whole day in and out of term time.

The child of two or three can attend a nursery school either full time or part time or can spend between one and ten sessions a week at a playgroup. Setting up a private playgroup or nursery school requires less funds than a creche, day nursery or workplace nursery.

Definitions

Playgroup

A playgroup offers sessional care to two- to five-year-olds attending alone or with their parents for not more than four hours a session. Most children start between the ages of two and three for a few mornings or afternoons a week. As the child grows older he or she can attend for five mornings or afternoons a week. This facility allows children to play together. They can participate in a range of activities from painting, modelling and cooking to dressing up, making jigsaws and singing. There are no lessons. The emphasis is on socialising and play. Children learn to interact with other children and other adults at playgroup.

A playgroup usually meets in a church hall, a private house or converted premises. Finding premises is perhaps one of the hardest tasks for the new playgroup proprietor. Those who can use their own home are in a strong position and stand a chance of making a profit more quickly than those paying rent or mortgage repayments. Playgroup usually meets during term time only. It is often run by its proprietors with additional paid help to maintain the correct child to helper ratio.

This is a potential growth area in the small business sector. Many non-working mothers can afford a limited amount of child care; this is the perfect solution. The child leaves his or her own home, giving the mother time to do something quietly at home, devote more time to a younger child, or go out, and the child is mixing with other children in a different environment. He or she plays with different toys, can do messy things perhaps not allowed at home, and begins to develop a sense of independence.

Some playgroups are run by registered childminders or nannies. For instance, an employer with a large home might not want to lose a nanny, so might come to an arrangement to turn over part of the house for use as a playgroup offering sessional care to other children as well as her own. If this is the case, the nanny ought to have the same share in the business as her employer.

All prospective playgroup owners will benefit enormously from the help given by the Pre-school Playgroups Association (PPA). Further information is given in Chapter 7.

Extended day playgroup

There is a trend towards extended day playgroups. This means that a child can attend both the morning and afternoon sessions, freeing the parents to work full time. Lunch can be provided by the playgroup; otherwise a child staying for the entire day is asked to bring a packed lunch. Some childminders or nannies might find it easier to set up an extended day playgroup perhaps for three children at first, since they will have experience of looking after one child for the entire day.

Parent and toddler group

A parent and toddler group comprises children who are always accompanied by an adult who stays for the complete session. It is unlikely that this service will make a profit. More space is required and the fees charged are low. This facility is usually run by members of the community including parents, so it is not discussed here. But go ahead and set up a group in your area if you think there is a need. Parents will probably help on a rota system and will not expect to be paid. Daily fees can still be kept to a minimum (make a small charge for tea or coffee). If you pay only a low rent, perhaps for a church hall, you might be able to take a small salary for yourself. Some groups have now been renamed carer and toddler groups or adult and toddler groups to include childminders and nannies.

Under-fives group

An under-fives group is a combined adult and toddler group and playgroup. Some children, usually those under the age of three, are accompanied by an adult and others are not. Again, this is not discussed further but do set one up if there is the demand.

Toy library

A toy library promotes the principle that play matters for the developing child. It bridges the gap in the existing provision for families with babies and young children and for people with special needs. Providing play opportunities and enhancing children's play experience are a major part of the toy library's function. It can be compared with a children's library; books are borrowed from or read in a library, whereas toys, and books are played with or borrowed from a toy library. In addition, there is greater social interaction. The opportunity exists for carers and parents to meet in much the same way as at an under-fives group or playgroup.

Most of the current groups are voluntary organisations but there are possibilities for a privately funded toy library. If you feel there is a need in your area, go ahead. Playmatters/The National Toy Libraries Association will supply information.

Nursery school

A nursery school is defined as an establishment attended regularly by a child so that he or she can participate in educational activities. It must have in its employ one or more trained nursery/infant teachers. To all intents and purposes a nursery school is a playgroup, but instead of having the emphasis completely on play, lessons, pre-reading and number work are introduced for the older children. This is a good service for working parents. Children over three can attend from 9.00 am to 3.30 pm but some attend in the mornings or afternoons only until they are ready to stay for the whole day. Most nursery schools operate during term time only. A parent who cannot collect a child at 3.30 pm can arrange for a minder, friend or relative to do so. If the parent works, the minder could also care for the child during the holidays.

After the first few years, when all profits are ploughed back into the business to buy equipment, etc, this business can provide the proprietors with a reasonable income. The ratio of employees to children does not make the total salary bill prohibitive, and some parents will often pay higher fees if their child can learn more than at playgroup. The afternoon session could be extended and higher fees charged. Working parents could then collect their own children after work. Again, the lack of premises in some areas limits the number of new nursery schools.

Montessori nursery school

A Montessori nursery school is one that uses the Montessori approach to teaching. This approach is child centred. The trained Montessori teacher guides and directs the children in a carefully planned and structured environment allowing freedom of choice and expression. Writing and Montessori reading and arithmetic are taught, and usually one or more projects on history, geography or biology, etc are run each term. Art and drama also form an important part of the curriculum. Montessori materials such as sandpaper letters, numerals, factor boards and knobbed cylinders are introduced. The Montessori Equipment Company will send you a catalogue of equipment available. It can also give advice on how to start a Montessori nursery school.

Day nursery

A day nursery provides full-time care for children from the age of six weeks to five years. It is usually open for most of the year. This facility is nearly always used by working parents. Children can stay until 6.00pm to enable parents to do a full day's work. The day nursery whose prime aim is care and protection is not without an educational function, though.

If the nursery restricts ages to between two-and-a-half and five years and provides care for four hours or more a day for each child, it become a day care group.

Creche

A creche can accommodate children of any age provided that the parent or carer is on the premises. This is a necessary requirement for a valid insurance policy. In every other respect a creche functions as a day nursery. The majority of creches are provided by private employers.

However, many one-off or short-term creches are run as voluntary groups. A creche may be available for a few hours while a meeting or lecture is held or over a period of several months during a course.

This need not be the case. In fact, privately funded creches at computer shows, small business shows, fêtes, swimming baths, health clubs, even in restaurants or large shopping centres, would be most welcome. These short-term or one-off creches must recruit experienced helpers, since there will always be a flux of children. Often children will only attend once. It is helpful if a core of children can be encouraged to attend regularly each week over the period the creche is up and running.

The Oxford Creche Development Project produces *Guidelines for Good Practice in Creches* which covers all aspects of setting up and running a creche including a one-off creche.

Gingerbread produces a guide for local community groups entitled *Starting a Creche*. It will be of help to privately funded creches too.

Workplace nursery

A workplace nursery is a day nursery to meet the needs of working parents and the social, educational and welfare needs of their children. Many are run by large companies for their employees' children. To make up the numbers some take children from the community. The nursery can be on the company's premises or on a separate site. More and more large companies are introducing workplace nurseries as a benefit for employees with children. Workplace Nurseries exists to help its members (annual membership £10, 1989/90) on many aspects of work-related child care.

The National and Local Government Officers' Association (NALGO) has published on workplace nurseries. It also produces a booklet entitled *Organising a Creche*.

Babysitting

Babysitting agencies, clubs and circles are not covered in this book. Setting up an agency is completely different. This falls under the heading of employment agency which must be licensed annually by the Department of Employment.

Camp, playscheme or franchise

Camps and playschemes are usually for older children. They are often run out of school hours. The National Out of School Alliance (NOOSA) deals with school-age children. It helps groups providing play and care for this age group. Contact NOOSA if you are thinking of setting up a scheme during the school holidays, perhaps in conjunction with a training programme for parents.

One franchise that provides a facility for pre-school children is Tumble Tots. It is an exciting new active physical play programme. Becoming a Tumble Tots licensee is not cheap. The total amount you will require is £4500 plus VAT. Each licensee is supplied with equipment worth £2000, trained and helped with the initial classes. Premises of between 1200 and 1800 square feet must be found and hired by the licensee. If you are interested, ring the National Licensing Controller.

Classes are held once a week for 40 to 45 minutes for each age group from birth to six years. Advertisements in the local press and being part of a large organisation should help you to recruit children. However, classes held three or four mornings or afternoons a week at several halls are necessary to make a reasonable profit.

Since finding premises is often the hardest part of setting up any child care business, once you have secured the lease of a hall it might be better to invest the above amount in setting up a privately funded playgroup. You won't have the support of the parent organisation but you will have the support of the PPA. A small playgroup in London employing two playgroup leaders during its start-up year, 1987/88, had a turnover of £5000!

Part-time or full-time care and how many children?

Having read the above definitions you may have decided on your choice of child care business. Now think about the size you wish the operation to be. It is easier to register a small playgroup offering 12 places for five sessions a week than a day nursery taking many babies and open throughout the working day. However, the change in numbers or hours means that your licence will have to be approved and changed by the Social Services Department of your local authority. Small playgroups also cost less to set up, especially if a local hall is vacant and available at a reasonable rent. Premises can set the criteria for your playgroup or nursery. But you must take into account your market. What percentage of mothers in your area work? Working mothers may require a nursery of some kind for their children. Mothers who stay at home may wish to spend more time with their children and have less money to spend on child care. So they may require a playgroup or only a few sessions a week at nursery school for their over-threes. Is your business in the country, town or suburbs? How large is the catchment area?

Throughout this book 'playgroup or nursery' is used to refer to any place where children can attend outside home with people paid to take care of them. If a specific type of child care facility is mentioned, the appropriate term given in this chapter is used.

Chapter 3

Finance and Premises

Do you have a business of your own? Have you ever had a business of your own? Has your partner some experience of setting up a small business? This chapter assumes the answers to these questions are no. The procedures to help you set up a privately funded playgroup or nursery are described below.

A scheme of things to do

- type of playgroup or nursery
- choice of name
- number of proprietors
- business identity
- finance
- premises
- registration with Social Services
- insurance
- names of children for waiting list
- hire of helpers

Nearly all these points must be considered at the same time, so order of priority is hard to establish. Premises may have to be taken before you can apply for registration. The type of facility may be determined by the type of premises available. Almost everything will have to be done at once after your choice of partners, if any, and accumulation of part or all of the funds. You may have to work very quickly to find suitable premises, so be prepared for this. You may have to make arrangements for your own children to be looked after out of school hours because everything may have to be done between exchange and completion of contracts on a property. To get preliminary answers it may be better to visit some people yourself. Be prepared to be kept waiting on the telephone when making enquiries. Anticipate a large quarterly bill.

Finance

It would be foolish to set up a small business with no capital of your own. At times of high interest rates it is unwise to borrow the full amount. A small amount of savings or collateral may suffice. You may, however, have to match every pound borrowed with a pound of your savings. Taking on a partner who has some money to invest should be considered.

Prepare a sound business plan and cash-flow forecast before proceeding. First, assess the size and nature of your business. If the number of children falls, will the number of helpers employed have to be reduced to recoup some of the lost revenue? Build these possible losses into your forecast.

First make a list of the overheads for your business. It will probably resemble the list given below. Then fill in an amount for each category for months 1 to 12. Let month 1 be the month in which you start your small business. You may have to guess some amounts.

Overheads

	months				
	1	2	3	...	12
rent					
rates (including water)					
gas					
electricity					
heating					
telephone					
insurance					
stationery					
postage					
local advertising					
van or car services					
maintenance					
bank interest (overdraft)					
bank charges					
total overheads					

A cash-flow forecast shows the amount of money a business expects in a particular month. Receipts and payments will not be evenly spaced over the 12-month period. The balance at the beginning of each term, September, January and April, will be higher than other months for any playgroup or nursery billing parents termly. Now using figures for overheads complete the cash-flow forecast for months 1 to 12.

Cash-flow forecast

	months 1	2	3	...	12
balance at beginning of month					
fees received					
payments					
trade creditors					
overheads					
other payments					
assets bought					
balance					
overdraft					

Now prepare a profit and loss account for the first 12 months of trading, or prepare one for each quarterly period if you wish. The break-even point is reached when income equals expenditure.

Profit and loss account

		£
	gross profit	
fees forecast		
other income		
direct costs		
labour		
materials		
	total overheads	
	loss/profit	

Building society mortgage or bank loan?

A building society could be approached for a mortgage. It might be easier to buy a large property that can be easily split into living quarters and nursery school or playgroup and get a joint home/business mortgage. You will be asked to provide a larger deposit and pay a slightly higher rate of interest than usual. But if you are married, your husband's salary can be used to secure the mortgage.

The following rates change as the economy changes its status. Familiarise yourself with the different kinds of rate.

mortgage rate
bank base rate
bank prime overdraft rate
personal loan rate

credit card rate
hire purchase rate
bank deposit account rate
building society ordinary account rate
high-interest cheque account rate
inflation rate

Current figures can be found in the money sections of some daily newspapers, for example:

- Family Money in the Money section of the Saturday edition of *The Times*
- Money Mail in the *Daily Mail*
- Money in the Saturday edition of *The Independent*
- Family Money in the Saturday edition of the *Telegraph*

Some papers even give the best buys of the week for borrowers.

If your husband is a high earner, both you and your husband could jointly and severally guarantee a loan for premises away from your home. The bank's money is guaranteed if the business fails; your husband can repay the loan from his salary. If you borrow money to invest in your business, tax relief is available on the interest paid.

Grants

Grants may be one way of partially funding your playgroup or nursery. English Heritage publishes a book entitled *Directory of Public Sources of Grants for Repair and Conversion of Historic Buildings* which is available from their publications branch. Bodies such as local authorities, the Rural Development Commission (formerly CoSIRA), your city task force, the EC, the Department of Trade and Industry, the Ministry of Agriculture, the Training Agency (formerly the Manpower Services Commission) and the Sports Council might help to finance your venture. The addresses and telephone numbers appear in Chapter 14. Telephone the numbers relevant to your area, then send a few follow-up letters. Some grant assessors are motivated by the prospects for generating employment or creating business. The Department of the Environment is interested in inner cities urban development and regeneration, so if your playgroup or nursery is in one of these areas it might be willing to help you.

As a privately run playgroup or nursery it is more than likely that you will have to raise all funds yourself or rely on those of a partner. But if you speak to people, some avenues may open for you - perhaps a loan instead of a grant. If you are between the ages of 18 and 25, submit a proposal, business plan and completed application form to the Prince's Youth Business Trust. You may be lucky enough to get a loan of up to £5000 and a grant of £1000 for equipment. The Trust likes applicants to show initiative, such as obtaining a bank loan first. Ring the head office to obtain the name and telephone number of your regional coordinator.

Government schemes

The government's Business Expansion Scheme allows an investor, under certain conditions, to buy a shareholding in a playgroup or nursery and at the same time obtain tax relief on the investment, left untouched for five years, at the higher rate of 40 per cent if a high tax payer. One example written up in *The Times* is a nursery-to-prep school in St John's Wood, London. First, the proprietor found the premises, then sought the finance. She secured a large mortgage. A prospectus was drawn up for potential investors through the Business Expansion Scheme. Forecasts were presented and it was clear that the school could not achieve a profit in its first year. Investors were attracted and an amount of money close to the ceiling set by the government was raised. Perks were offered in the form of a discount on school fees for any child of their choice if shareholders took up a large number of shares. This is a tale on a grand scale but it does illustrate the point.

A smaller nursery hoping to take fewer children could do the same. However, it is unwise to give perks such as subsidised places to investor-nominated children or those of helpers. Maximum revenue will be used in the early years. Helpers may even be required to work for lower wages for the first year to make ends meet. After one year, though, salaries could be brought to scale for the qualification held.

The government pays £40 a week for one year under its Enterprise Allowance Scheme for those setting up a new business. The only criteria are that the person has been drawing unemployment benefit for eight weeks or more and has £1000 to invest in the business. She must not start the business before being accepted on to the Scheme. More information is available from Jobcentres.

The government and the banks together can also help a small business through their business Loan Guarantee Scheme. Use as a last resort, since it is expensive. The government will provide guarantees on sums up to £75,000 but at a high rate of interest.

The approach should be made through your bank.

Agencies offering advice

Local enterprise agencies give advice such as how to prepare a business plan. There are 300 offices throughout the country. Addresses and telephone numbers can be obtained from Business in the Community and in Scotland from Scottish Business in the Community. This is a free service. Some areas of the country have been designated Enterprise Zones. If your playgroup or nursery falls within one of them, you might be entitled to some extra help.

The Small Firms Service will provide information free at the initial visit but a small fee is charged at subsequent visits. To contact your local Small Firms Centre dial 100 and ask the operator for Freefone Enterprise.

Local authorities can be extremely helpful. All the telephone numbers for your area can be found in a copy of *The Social Services Yearbook* (Longman) which will be in the reference section of your public library, or in your local telephone directory.

Premises: layout of playgroup or nursery

The lack of reasonably priced premises to rent seems to be a country-wide problem. Two rooms 1000 square feet in total, a kitchen and two loos for any facility other than a playgroup offering part-time care should be considered as the minimum. If there is a choice of halls or other rented premises, take the one on the less busy road.

A playgroup in a private dwelling may consist of a large room, loos, a kitchen and a small garden. Often playgroups housed in church halls have little say with regard to layout; they are presented with a large airy hall, a kitchen at one end and loos at the other. But it may have the advantage of a church garden. A garden shed could be erected to store pushalongs, bikes and a climbing frame. Children should have access to outdoor play equipment. A purpose-built nursery is large and has been designed for the ages and needs of the children who will use it. An area of 40 square feet per child (for those under one staying all day) is considered usual.

When designing and arranging the equipment in a playgroup or nursery the golden rule is to separate noisy activities from quiet ones. The layouts below are not drawn to scale.

Playgroup housed in a church hall

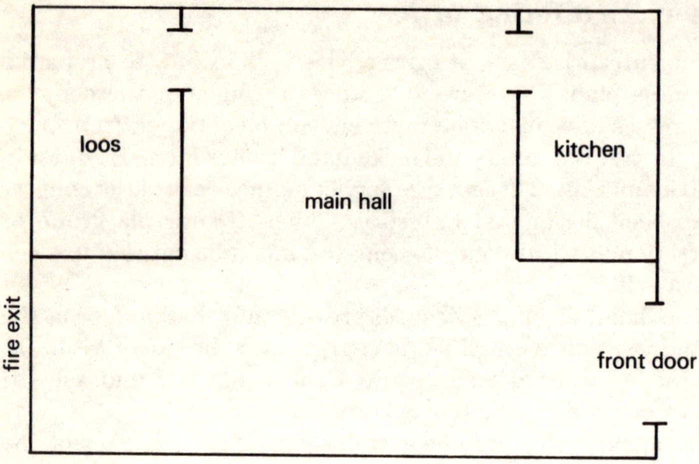

Nursery school

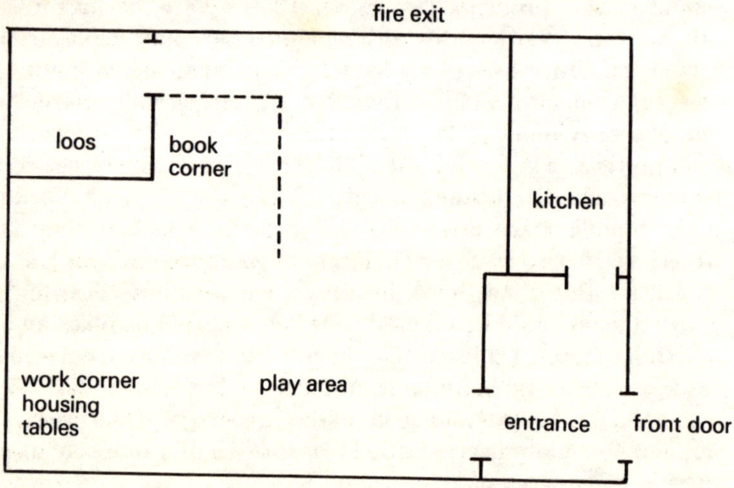

Purpose-built day nursery

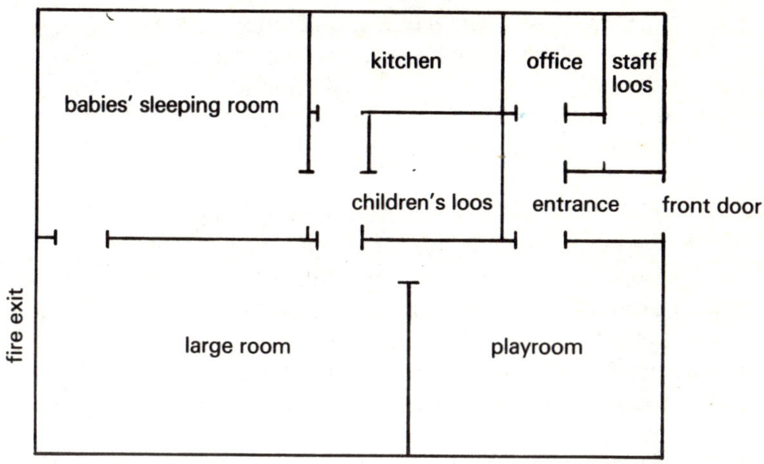

Business identity

Do you intend to work alone with only paid helpers? If so, being a sole trader may be sufficient. However, if you plan to take one or more partners, the choice between a partnership, limited company or cooperative must be made. By far the majority of businesses in Britain employ fewer than 25 people and there are many excellent books on forming a small business. Consult the reference section of your public library. Kogan Page has published at length on this subject, so write for a publications list. Chapter 10 takes each of these categories with respect to opening a bank account.

Limited companies involve more detailed accounting and auditing procedures but they pay corporation tax on profits under £150,000 at 25 per cent, 15 per cent less than individuals paying higher rate income tax, and offer limited liability.

Limited liability means that your creditors cannot take your home or other personal possessions if your business fails. This may be a good idea if you have sufficient funds to get started. But if you plan to borrow part or all of this amount a small business, limited company or not, may have to give a personal guarantee, jointly and severally, perhaps between husband and wife.

A partnership ought to have a written agreement legally drawn up and it does not enjoy limited liability.

Registration

All playgroups, nurseries, nursery schools, creches and workplace nurseries (with the exclusion of those run in hospitals) must register with the Social Services Department of their local authority under the Nurseries and Childminders Regulation Act 1948 as amended by the Health Services and Public Health Act 1968. The 1948 act states:

Every local health authority shall keep registers:
of premises in their area, other than premises wholly or mainly used as private dwellings where children are received to be looked after for the day or a substantial part thereof for any longer period not exceeding six days;
of persons in their area who for reward receive into their homes children under the age of five to be looked after as aforesaid.

Each local authority has the power to impose maximum number of children, qualifications of those in charge, staffing - qualifications, experience, numbers - medical supervision of children, standards of accommodation, equipment, feeding and diet. Those who fail to register are breaking the law. The 1968 amendment was to include care of more than two hours a day.

As soon as possible speak to your pre-school adviser, underfives officer, under-fives coordinator, or person in charge of day care for the under-fives at the Social Services Department of your local authority, often based in the Town Hall. Ask for a form to register a private playgroup or nursery. Most forms are self-explanatory, incorporating a comprehensive notes section. A brief description of accommodation, names and qualifications of helpers and proprietors, fees charged to parents, meals served and records kept (such as an accident book and a daily register) must be recorded. The procedures for acceptance and the vetting of helpers employed are similar to those described for a childminder in Chapter 11. Once registration has been approved you will be told of the maximum number of children you can take, your hours of opening, the ratio of children to each helper (Chapter 4) and any other important information. It is necessary to inform Social Services each time a helper leaves your employment and a new one starts.

A name

Choose a name for your new or newly acquired playgroup or

nursery. Have a brightly coloured sign painted and place it in a prominent position. Under the Companies Act 1981 all privately run playgroups and nurseries trading under a name other than that of its proprietors must display at the site of the playgroup or nursery and on all business stationery the proprietors' names and an address for correspondence for each proprietor. Failure to comply is a criminal offence and may affect any contracts or agreements between the proprietors and a third party.

Fire regulations

The fire officer will check your playgroup or nursery carefully to ensure that it complies with fire regulation standards. Contact the Fire Services as soon as possible, since it is likely that some alterations will have to be made. These could delay registration with the Social Services Department and put back the date on which you can open.

Number of children to one loo

The ratio is laid down by the Social Services Department of your local authority, so get it right before refitting commences. These facilities should be modern and of a high standard. Easy access is important, too. It is wise if all paintwork is washable. Children favour bright colours.

Building conversion and planning permission

Some playgroups and nurseries may be advised that they need planning permission, even in a church hall. Check with the local authority planning department before buying or renting premises. Talk to the development control officer. A Section 53 Determination letter to the planning authority to determine whether planning permission is necessary will clarify the situation. From shop to nursery may require permission for a change of use. Any building work should be carried out by a member of the Federation of Master Builders. Only agree a price once you have received a written estimate.

Outdoor facilities

An outdoor play area must be taken if the premises offer it. Many, such as community halls, do not have this facility. This can be a major drawback to a new business attracting parents and children as access to outdoor play equipment is important.

Buying a playgroup or nursery

Occasionally an advertisement appears in *The Times* on the Independent Education page offering a nursery school for sale. For example, a nursery incorporating living accommodation in an area two hours' commuting time north of London with a £30,000 turnover per annum might be on the market for £115,000. This price may seem high if the cost of a similar sized property in your area is £20,000 less. If the nursery has been adapted to meet all planning requirements, if there is a list of children who are willing to attend the nursery under new management, and if all the equipment is included, this could be an excellent price. Do your research thoroughly before putting in an offer. Get the opinion of local residents. Try to discover any drawbacks. Is the owner selling for personal reasons such as retirement, relocation because of husband's job, or for a change of career? Or is it for business reasons? If the answer to the last question is yes, determine why the business was not a success. Only buy if you are confident that you can overcome any problems. Ask to see the audited accounts for the three years previous to the sale and get somebody other than yourself or your partner to look over them. Take the advice of more than one solicitor, accountant, bank manager and chartered surveyor. *The Solicitors' Regional Directory 1988*, giving details of local solicitors, solicitors who do legal aid work, and those who offer a fixed fee interview for not more than £5, is published by the Law Society. If you know an accountant or successful businessman, ask for an unbiased opinion. Always commission a full structural survey on any property you might buy.

Other places to look for nursery schools or day nurseries on the market are the property pages of local papers, evening papers, *Exchange & Mart*, *Dalton's Weekly*, the *Guardian*, and *Nursery World*.

Chapter 4

Getting and Keeping Helpers

All aspects of hiring staff for privately funded playgroups and nurseries are discussed here.

A prerequisite for the job is to like working with children. Young children are often noisy and unpredictable, so patience, energy, flexibility and imagination are other qualities to look for when hiring people. If the playgroup or nursery is still in its first year, an inordinate amount of energy will be required. When choosing a team be sure that the different personalities, including your own, will complement each other when taken together. There is nothing worse for group morale if one member of the team does less than her fair share.

Having decided upon the type of business you wish to offer, found suitable premises, opened a bank account, generated start-up funds and registered with the Social Services Department of your local authority, you must now decide upon the number and level of helpers you need to employ, if any. It is important that under-fives are adequately supervised, so child to helper ratios are given below, together with a list of useful child care qualifications. More details of courses are given in Chapter 12.

Child to helper ratio

The child to helper ratios for all types of playgroup or nursery are laid down by the Social Services Department of your local authority. They vary from region to region but here is a general rule.

Playgroup

Five to eight children to one helper (5:1 to 8:1) for children aged two-and-a-half to five years attending a privately funded playgroup for five to ten sessions a week is usual. Each session can last for three-and-a-half hours. There is no legal requirement for staff to be trained. However, some playgroups open for five mornings a week only and sessions are two-and-a-half hours long. The earliest age at which a child can be admitted to playgroup or nursery varies throughout the country. For example, children attending groups in some London boroughs can do so from the age of two. Those taking up a place in Hampshire must wait until their third birthday.

Nursery
The ratio is usually five to eight children to one helper (5:1 to 8:1) for children aged two-and-a-half to five years attending a privately funded nursery for five to ten sessions a week. Each session can last for three-and-a-half hours. Again there is no legal requirement for staff to be trained. A nursery can only be registered as a nursery school if it has one or more trained nursery/infant teachers in its employ.

Day nursery
If children aged two-and-a-half to five years attend a private day nursery to which the parents pay fees, the child to helper ratio is often 6:1 plus a supervisor. Times vary but usually full-time care is offered. Once again there is no legal requirement for staff to be trained. Many day nurseries take babies. An increase in the numbers of babies or children under 18 months means that it is mandatory in some regions for more helpers to be employed. Some local authorities say that the ratio should be adjusted to 2:1 or 3:1 for these children and that all helpers be trained nursery nurses. Others promote the care of babies and young toddlers in a home environment by a childminder.

Creche and workplace nursery
A privately funded creche that takes, for example, 24 children from six weeks of age ought to have at least five helpers and one supervisor. Again, more staff must be employed if there is a very high proportion of babies attending. Hours are flexible. There is no legal requirement for staff to be trained.

Childminding
Are you thinking of childminding under-fives to gain experience before setting up your own playgroup or nursery? If so, the ratio is three children to one minder (3:1). This ratio must include your own children if they are under five years of age. The minded child can attend for eight hours a day, 52 weeks a year if there is a need.

Having applied for registration you will be supplied with specific regulations by the Social Services Department of your local authority that must be fulfilled before you can run a playgroup or nursery in your area. Non-profit making groups registered as charities to all intents and purposes are treated in the same way as privately funded organisations. However, the public sector, or statutory groups as they are known, has to fulfil strict conditions.

Child care qualifications

It is possible to set up a private playgroup or nursery employing helpers not trained in child care. However, unless the proprietors have some experience in child care it would be foolish to do so. Colleges running child care courses in your area can be very helpful when you are setting up and looking for helpers, so be sure to contact them. Here is a list of child care qualifications.

- National Nursery Examination Board (NNEB) Certificate

Nursery nurses with the award of the NNEB are very much in demand in nursery schools, creches, day nurseries and in some playgroups. They have been well trained in child care, are usually very committed to the nursery and the children, and they do not command a high wage.

- Scottish Nursery Nurses' Board (SNNB) registration

Registration with the SNNB is the Scottish equivalent of the award of the NNEB. It has superseded the Scottish Nursery Nurses' Examination Board (SNNEB) Certificate.

- The Business and Technician Education Council (BTEC) National Diploma in Caring Services (Nursery Nursing)

A helper with this BTEC qualification has also been well trained in child care. This qualification is slowly being recognised as an alternative to the award of the NNEB.

- London Montessori Centre Nursery (Foundation) Teaching Diploma
- London Montessori Centre NNEB and Child Care and Teaching Diploma
- St Nicholas Montessori College Diploma

If you are setting up or buying an existing Montessori school, some of your helpers should hold one or other of these qualifications. Support services, such as workshops, given by the London Montessori Centre and St Nicholas Montessori College will prove invaluable.

- Chiltern Nursery Training College Child Care Certificate
- Norland Preliminary Certificate
- Norland Diploma and Badge
- Princess Christian Certificate

Most nannies study first for the award of the NNEB and the Royal Society of Health Diploma of Nursery Nursing at these private colleges. Upon graduation they can command high salaries when working for families but a nanny might wish to work in a playgroup or nursery for other reasons. A nursery in an affluent suburb may benefit from having a few trained nannies as helpers simply because some parents have heard of the qualification and are impressed by it.

- Registered General Nurse (RGN)
- Registered Sick Children's Nurse (RSCN)

Both these qualifications are appropriate for helpers in day nurseries where children remain for long periods each day. They might reassure some parents leaving babies in the care of the nursery and therefore might give it an advantage over another nearby nursery employing less well-qualified staff.

- Certificate of Education in Nursery Teaching
- Certificate of Education in Infant Teaching

These are necessary qualifications for the nursery school helper. If you have started or taken over a nursery school which conducts lessons in skills such as basic letter and number recognition, writing and pre-reading work, and puts very little emphasis on play, one or more helpers holding one or other of these qualifications must be employed.

- PPA foundation course
- PPA advanced course
- PPA field workers course

The many branches of the Pre-school Playgroups Association (PPA) run these courses for playgroup leaders. Qualifications are not recognised nationally but they are highly thought of and are useful to those running playgroups. Those who have been awarded the PPA certificate of assessment for the foundation course have observed children, conducted a child study and completed practical projects, in addition to having visited institutions involved in the care and education of under-fives. Some local authorities favour PPA qualifications for their playgroup helpers.

Selection

Advertising a post

If you have been trained in some aspect of child care and if your partner has an appropriate qualification, and if you both intend to work in the playgroup or nursery, you might only need to employ a school-leaver. This will save you money. However, it is not always possible to do everything yourself, especially if you have children of your own. A small nursery taking 12 children per session might need to employ two helpers, and at least one should have a qualification in child care. Playgroups which open for five morning sessions and charge only £2 per child per session will almost certainly have to employ untrained helpers. In order to minimise costs parents might be encouraged to do a duty, say, once every three weeks. A helper must never be on her own with the children in a playgroup or nursery. This is extremely important in all groups and must be adhered to at all times.

When looking for helpers for your playgroup or nursery you could place an advertisement in *Nursery World*, in *Nursing Times* if you are looking for a nurse specifically, in *The Times Educational Supplement* if you wish to employ a teacher and in your local paper.

Contact any of the colleges running NNEB courses and ask the course organiser to mention the job vacancy to those students who are near the end of, or have completed, their course. The course organiser might also be persuaded to place a written advertisement on the notice board. Some colleges supply a list of job vacancies to their students. They might include your vacancy in their list. The same applies to the colleges that run the BTEC National Diploma in Caring Services (Nursery Nursing). Telephone or write to your regional office of the PPA to ask for the address of the nearest adult education centre that runs PPA courses. Contact the centre in case any playgroup leaders who have completed a course are looking for employment.

Post advertisements in places where nannies, students, etc

meet and in local primary schools. Libraries might generate a good response to an advertisement especially if there is a children's library in the same builing. Cards carrying the advertisement could also be put in your local post office, newsagents or corner shop window. Give your local Jobcentre details of vacancies. It is always easier if helpers live locally, especially if they have school-age children.

If you want to attract school-leavers specifically, write to your nearest secondary school with a copy of the advertisement, asking the head teacher to let you know who is interested, a prospective college student with a year to spare, for example. This can also be a route to getting some volunteer help. Again, ask the head teacher.

Interview

Once you have received sufficient replies to your advertisement, compile a list of interviewees. See everyone if you wish. But a short list of six is sufficient to choose from.

You should have selected an interviewing committee of any partners in the business, a couple of parents (optional) and a field worker if you feel you need some help. The fact that the interviewee arrives punctually (or not as the case may be) gives an indication whether she will be a good timekeeper.

Having set the interviews for a good time for the children if the playgroup or nursery is already open, let the interviewee speak to the children, meet the other helpers and see the range of equipment. Then conduct a formal interview in a separate room. Put the interviewee at ease first, perhaps by asking about her own children or her journey to the playgroup or nursery.

It is often helpful to prepare a list of questions beforehand. Try to ask questions that do not require yes/no answers. For example, begin questions with what, where, when. Let the interviewee do most of the talking. Does the candidate have any special abilities that would be useful to the playgroup or nursery? Will she fit in with the rest of the team?

After checking that she is physically up to the job, has the correct qualifications and interests, make sure her domestic situation will not affect her work. For instance, if she has a school-age child and nursery staff are expected to start work at 8.30 am, be sure that she can make arrangements for her child to get to school in time for her to get to work at 8.30 am. The same applies to collection from school. To close the interview you could present the candidate with a copy of the job description, ask her opinion of the job, whether she would make any changes, and whether she has any other questions to ask.

If the candidate is already employed, find out how much notice she must give her present employer and ask for a written reference. This is crucial if you are working to a tight schedule, and if, for example, the playgroup or nursery is expected to open in a few weeks' time.

You may wish to employ an RGN or a certified nursery/infant teacher instead of a nursery nurse or playgroup leader, but the selection procedure remains the same. However, if the job vacancy is for a school-leaver with no experience, some of the above points will not be relevant; instead quiz the candidate on further education and her willingness to do a part-time course in child care.

Job description

Devise a job description for each category of helper. If your playgroup or nursery is new, draw up a brief job description for a nursery worker or helper. This description can be amended and broken down into more than one job description as the nursery develops. The Professional Association of Nursery Nurses' (PANN) working party 'Nursery Nurses in Education' has produced a job description for all nursery nurses in nursery schools. Write to the association for it. A useful pamphlet *Nursery Nursing: A Life with Children* is published by the NNEB. Write to the National Association of Certificated Nursery Nurses (NACNN) if you want more help with specific questions. The PPA also produces a job description for playgroup leaders. On page 36 is a short specimen job description for a nursery school helper.

Job description for a nursery school helper

1. To arrive at 8.30 am to set up the apparatus for the morning session (9.00 am to 12.30 pm) and to leave only after clearing away after the afternoon session (12.00 to 3.30 pm) encouraging the children to help in these activities.
2. To supervise children indoors including during lunch and breaks and outdoors during play or outings or other activities.
3. To maintain records, registers, books, materials, equipment, first aid box, etc.
4. To maintain non-racial and non-sexist discrimination at all times and to provide ethnic playing and learning facilities and to consider different diets and religious practices.
5. To welcome parents or carers, encourage them to help in fund-raising activities and consult and advise them when necessary.
6. To act as a parent figure to the children throughout the session.
7. To administer basic first aid and stay with a sick child until a parent or carer arrives, providing a safe environment at all times.
8. To work as part of a team and to attend staff meetings and other meetings and to do other necessary chores outside working hours.
9. To encourage the cognitive development and social skills of the children by reading to them, introducing puzzles and games, play, number recognition, and supervising drawing and pre-reading work.
10. To cover for staff when sick or attending courses.

Other points to include could be to attend specific courses, order consumables, clean the kitchen, etc. But if your playgroup or nursery is new, you may wish to do certain things yourself. So think carefully before writing the job description, jotting down ideas on a piece of paper over the course of a week. Be sure to state any specific conditions. As mentioned above, it is good if the job description evolves with the business; the areas of emphasis might not be apparent immediately. Again the emphasis will be determined by the category of helpers employed and the daily procedures in your playgroup or nursery.

Letter offering employment

Once the playgroup or nursery has decided upon a nursery nurse or playgroup leader, etc, a letter offering employment is sent to the successful candidate giving details of salary, working hours, job title, length of trial period, starting date and expectations. Here is an example of such a letter sent to a nursery nurse.

Letter offering employment

________________ Nursery School

(Address)

____

Telephone ________________

(Names and addresses of proprietors)

Liz Smith

____

____

____

30 March 1989

Dear Liz

The proprietors of __________ Nursery School would like to offer you the job of nursery nurse at _______________ (address) from 8.30 am to 4.00 pm each Monday to Friday during term time. The salary is £____ per annum. The post begins on Monday _____________. Our nursery school is open from 9.00 am to 3.30 pm and the time outside these hours is to be spent on preparation and clearing away.

This post carries a trial period of one term and at the end of this period a contract will be issued to you if everything is satisfactory.

I look forward to hearing from you and hope very much that you will accept this offer.

Yours sincerely

(name of proprietor)

Contract or letter of employment

A contract is usually presented to the member of staff once she has worked for a period of three months. If your playgroup or nursery is new and you do not wish to waste money paying the wrong helper for longer than necessary, you could hire someone for one month or even one week to see if she fits in. Pay her freelance rates if you wish. But be sure to state these conditions in the letter offering employment.

Contracts are a legal obligation for those helpers who work for more than 16 hours a week, and must be issued within 13 weeks of starting work. Fill in all the spaces on the contract. Write 'not applicable' or 'none' rather than leave an empty space. The contract must be presented to the employee not later than seven days after the date in para 1. Ask your helper to sign two copies of the contract. Keep one for yourself and give her the other copy.

An example of a contract or letter of employment is given on page 39. Print out or type your contract on to sheets of your headed paper.

Use this contract if you wish and amend it to suit your business. For example, change playgroup to nursery school, creche, day nursery or workplace nursery; playleader to nursery nurse, helper, nursery teacher, etc and playgroup committee's officials to proprietors.

Some standard contracts can be obtained from law publishers or stationers. The PPA will also supply this Sample Contract of Employment with Explanatory Notes free of charge to its members. A Sample Tenancy Agreement is also available. These can be obtained from the PPA National Centre. The Equal Opportunities Commission will help with legal requirements and regulations if you have any queries.

Registration of helpers

Like childminders all paid nursery or playgroup helpers need to be registered with the Social Services Department of your local authority. They should fill in a form for the private day care sector to comply with the Nurseries and Childminders Regulation Act 1948 as amended by the Health Services and Public Health Act 1968. Be sure to get a batch of these forms when you apply for registration. Your new member of staff must give details of health and any court offences or offences against children. She is then thoroughly vetted by Social Services, and her name is processed by the police computer.

Dismissal

A helper can be dismissed once a number of written warnings have been given. Always keep a copy of any written warnings. For instance, if there is unsatisfactory work or time keeping, etc, at least one written warning must be given to the helper in question. However, it is wise to give several written warnings over a period of time. If the situation continues and the children are suffering as a result, the employer can terminate the employment provided the correct amount of notice is given. This situation ought to be avoided if at all possible, since it is easier now than ever before for an employee to claim damages for wrongful dismissal. As an employer encourage your helpers to discuss any problems with you. If it is apparent that a helper is unhappy, it might be reflected in poor time keeping. If the problem cannot be alleviated, turn the situation around, perhaps by suggesting a new career or another playgroup or nursery, so that the employee resigns.

Gross misconduct (for example, theft or deliberate damage), however, can override this procedure.

Legislation

Your local Department of Employment office will supply leaflets on the Employment Protection Act 1975, Health and Safety at Work Act 1974, Redundancy Payments Act 1965 and Employment Act 1972. It will also help privately funded playgroups and nurseries to draw up their contract or letter of employment.

Employment Protection Act 1975

The Employment Protection Act 1975 gives certain employees automatic rights. A helper who

- works for 16 hours or more a week;
- has worked for 16 hours or more a week for at least two years but now works for eight hours or more a week;
- has worked for eight hours or more a week for five years;

is protected by this Act. These conditions are worth knowing, since some playgroups and nurseries are staffed entirely by part-time help. Under the Act these employees must be given

1. a contract or letter of employment clearly stating all conditions by the thirteenth week of service;

PRE-SCHOOL PLAYGROUPS ASSOCIATION
61–63 Kings Cross Road, London WC1X 9LL
STATEMENT OF TERMS AND CONDITIONS
OF EMPLOYMENT
*CONTRACTS OF EMPLOYMENT ACT 1972**

as amended by the Trade Union and Labour Relations Act 1974 and the Employment Protection Act 1975

1. THIS STATEMENT DATED ________________ SETS OUT CERTAIN PARTICULARS OF THE TERMS AND CONDITIONS ON WHICH
2. ____
   (Name of employer)
3. employs ________________________________
   (Name of employee)
4. (a) Your employment began with us on ____________ and, for the purpose of your individual rights as an employee, your previous employment with ____________________ counts as part of your continuous period of employment which therefore began on ____________________.

   (b) Your employment with us began on ______________. Your employment with your previous employer does not count as part of your continuous period of employment. (Delete (a) or (b) as appropriate)
5. You are employed as (insert job title) Playgroup ____________________.
6. (a) Scale or Rate of Remuneration or Method of calculating remuneration £ ____________

   (b) You are paid at ____________________ intervals
7. Normal hours of work (any other conditions relative to hours):
   From ________ am to ________ pm Mondays to Fridays
   From ________ am to ________ pm Mondays to Fridays
   except when ________________________ Primary School is closed for holidays.
8. Entitlement to holidays, including public holidays and holiday pay:
   Holidays will be the same as those for ______________ Primary School except ____________________
   Pay will continue/be suspended during holidays

* Reproduced by kind permission of the PPA.

9. Terms and conditions relating to incapacity due to sickness or injury and sick pay

____

(if none, say so)

10. Pensions and Pension Scheme

____

(if none, say so)

11. Amount of notice of termination to be given:
by employee ________ weeks by employer ________ weeks
When employee employed less than 2 years ________ weeks
When employee employed more than 2 years but less than 12, one week for each complete year with minimum of ________ weeks
When employee employed at least 12 years - 12 weeks.

12. THE ACT REQUIRES THAT YOU BE GIVEN THE FOLLOWING ADDITIONAL INFORMATION.
Disciplinary rules - The Playleader/s is responsible for the day-to-day running of the Playgroup, but is herself responsible to the Committee.
If dissatisfied with any disciplinary decision relating to you, you may raise the matter with the Playgroup __________ in writing.

13. Grievance procedure - The Playgroup Committee's officials will deal primarily with any grievance, but shall at the request of the person aggrieved refer the matter to the full Committee whose decision shall be binding.
If you wish to seek redress of any grievance you may have, you should raise the matter with the Playgroup ___________ in writing.

14. A contracting-out certificate under the Social Security Pensions Act 1975 is not in force in respect of employment to which this statement refers.

15. Other information:
    (1) Under the Health and Safety at Work Act 1974, it is the duty of all employees to conform to policy and safety codes of practice and to accept and carry out their responsibilities.
    (2) If the term of employment is for a fixed term of 2 years or more the right to a redundancy payment under the Redundancy Payments Act 1965 is hereby excluded.

Employee's signature to acknowledge receipt of this statement. ________________

Any changes in the above particulars must be notified within one month of the change.

2. a written statement of gross pay, deductions and net pay each pay day;
3. time off for job hunting or to arrange retraining if made redundant (after two years of employment);

4. maternity leave and the right to return to work after confinement;
5. statutory maternity pay (SMP) (see Chapter 10 for conditions);
6. compensation for unfair dismissal; however, a claim is unlikely if the proprietors follow the procedures laid down in the disciplinary procedure;
7. redundancy pay if the playgroup or nursery is forced to close; the proprietors must pay any helper one week's salary for each full year of service. If the helper is older than 41 years of age, she is entitled to one-and-a-half weeks' salary for each full year of service.

Health and Safety at Work Act 1974

The Health and Safety at Work Act 1974 imposes a duty on both the employer and employee to ensure the health, safety and welfare of those at a place of work. It states that the employer must provide safe premises for all employees. Read Chapter 8 on health and safety in playgroups and nurseries.

Supervision

The degree of supervision is dependent on the level of helper employed. A competent, experienced playgroup leader or nursery nurse might require very little supervision after the first two or three weeks. However, a school-leaver may be constantly asking questions and wanting reassurance.

Daily duties

The daily duties of playgroup or nursery helpers are described in Chapters 6 and 9.

Salaries

Helpers are often paid monthly by cheque. Part-time helpers or those who work freelance (for example, a nursery nurse from an agency) may wish to be paid weekly or daily in cash. Details on keeping a deductions working sheet for each helper, paying their National Insurance contributions and income tax, filling in a payslip, and completing annual tax returns pertaining to payments to helpers are given in Chapter 10.

Pre-school Playgroups Association (PPA)

The following rates are recommended by at least one London

branch of the PPA. (1988/89). The National Joint Council of Local Authorities has proposed scales for playgroup leaders. These hourly rates include a London weighting of £1395. Each session lasts for three-and-a-half hours.

1. Playgroup leader who has completed the PPA foundation course and received a certificate of assessment £9.28 per session for 40 weeks plus half pay for 12 weeks' holiday (ie six weeks' full pay)
   = £9.28 x 5 x 46 = £2134.40 = £177.87 per month.
2. Playgroup leader who has finished a PPA advanced course in addition to the PPA foundation course and received a certificate of assessment for each £11 per session for 40 weeks plus half pay for holidays
   = £11.00 x 5 x 46 = £2530.00 = £210.83 per month.
3. Playgroup leader who has not finished any PPA course £8 per session for 40 weeks plus half pay for holidays
   = £8.00 x 5 x 46 = £1840.00 = £153.33 per month.

An increase of 5 per cent is likely for 1989/90. In April 1988 a clothing allowance of £9.20 per month was introduced for each playgroup leader. This amount is not subject to income tax, and each playgroup leader must receive a separate cheque for this amount each month. Check with the Inland Revenue before you introduce such a scheme, so that each helper can receive the full benefit.

Professional Association of Nursery Nurses (PANN)
The annual salaries for nursery nurses in education given below were agreed by the National Joint Council for Local Authorities (1989/90).

Pay scale

(7)	£5772	(13)	£7335
(8)	£6129	(14)	£7509
(9)	£6513	(15)	£7692
(10/11)	£6918		
(12)	£7116		

Salaries are higher for officers in charge and for those working in residential or day nurseries who have additional qualifications. Try to attract good staff not by offering high salaries initially (unless you know you can afford to do so) but by offering good working conditions, flexibility, and perhaps a share of the profits from the second year onwards. Your major expenditure after your rent/mortgage repayments and rates is salaries. PANN will supply more detailed information if you telephone or write to them. These salaries are reviewed each year.

Chapter 5

Promotion and Advertising

Once premises have been found and you have decided upon a nursery, creche or playgroup and chosen a name, the next step is promotion and sales. This means attracting parents so that they enrol their children to start when the playgroup or nursery opens or place their names on a waiting list for a forthcoming term.

If the proprietors were previously working in a nursery it might be possible to take some children to the new nursery, but it is unlikely that all the available places will be filled in this way. A change of ownership, however, might mean that the playgroup or nursery has reached its full quota of children when the new proprietors start. The number of children enrolled will determine the income of the playgroup or nursery. For many groups their fees are the only source of income.

A new business can only benefit from publicity. It is extremely important for a nursery, creche or playgroup, however small, to project a good image. First, equip your playgroup or nursery with letterheaded stationery. Then write a press release and take a few photographs of your group. Expand the press release into a leaflet. Distribute your leaflets and send your press release to the free press and any local newspapers. Open days, parent visits and word of mouth recommendations can all increase business.

Letterheads and business stationery

A well-designed letterhead on good quality paper is essential for any small business. An appropriate choice of paper is Conquerer 100 gsm. If you do not use a word processor or computer for typing and printing out extra copies, it is better to choose white paper which photocopies better than coloured paper. White paper can be livened up by printing the letterhead in a colour or using black and an additional colour. For instance, print the name of the playgroup or nursery and its logo in red and its address and telephone number in black. Two-colour printing is more expensive than one, so be sure costs are within your budget. It might be better to spend the extra money on getting the logo designed and the layout of the page pleasing. If you know a commercial artist, typographer or paste-up artist, ask for some help with the design.

Choosing a logo is usually a matter of personal taste, rather like choosing a baby's name. Remember that the name and the logo ought to have a common theme. For example, in the leaflet on page 49 the name of the nursery school is the Apples Nursery School and its logo is an apple tree.

A nursery does not necessarily need printed invoices or business cards but it is wise to print compliments slips. Termly, monthly or weekly accounts for each child can be typed on headed paper. Many privately funded nurseries bill parents at the beginning of each term. A creche or workplace nursery that forms part of a large organisation, however, might benefit from printed invoices. These parents will most likely be billed once a month and may even have their fees deducted each month from their salary. Typing out a monthly invoice showing the amount paid by the employee and the employer's subsidy (if any) for each child in a 30-place nursery can take up valuable time.

Any of the high street printing franchises can supply you with headed paper and compliments slips, etc. Their prices are competitive and their turn-around time is short. They offer a design service, and will help you with page layout if you wish. Do not get the printing done until you are absolutely sure that the pasted up design is to your liking. When the printer presents you with 500 sheets of headed paper and you realise that you hate the design, you will be charged for printing regardless.

Once your initial order (of 500 sheets of headed paper and 500 compliment slips, for example) has been fulfilled, always ask for the original artwork to be returned. Keep this safely for your next printing order. You may wish to print a leaflet and it may be cheaper to have a good quality print (bromide) made of the logo, etc from your original artwork rather than have it redrawn and order new type.

Press release

A press release of your nursery, playgroup or creche is a short description of your facility that fits on to one sheet of paper. A sample press release for a small playgroup is given on page 47. It should be typed in double spacing, split into short paragraphs, with the most important information at the top. A contact name and number should be provided. Your local newspaper may reproduce it verbatim in full or in part, or publish a précis.

____________________ Playgroup

(Address)

____

____

Telephone ____________________

PRESS RELEASE

______ Playgroup opens on 4 January 1989. This playgroup is registered with the ______ Social Services Department for 16 children to attend the morning session (9.00 am–12.00 pm) and 16 the afternoon session (12.30 pm–3.30 pm). Open five days a week during term time only, it caters for two-and-a-half to five-year-olds.

Emphasis is put on play and social interaction but the older children are encouraged to learn their letters and numbers and to write their name.

Parents who would like to visit the group and enrol their child can do so on the first Tuesday of each month.

The proprietors, both trained nursery nurses, work alongside two paid playleaders to maintain a ratio of one helper to four children.

Further information is available if you telephone (name) on ________________.

Local press

It is helpful if you or one of the parents knows a reporter on your local paper; if not, ring the desk and ask for the reporter in charge of education and social services, and send the material to him or her; try to make personal contact. Apart from sending out a press release to the editor or a contact, send some photographs as well. Paste captions on the back for identification purposes – the paper will receive a great many.

When you have some children in the playgroup, you may be able to persuade the newspaper to write an editorial on your group, especially if it is new to the area or under new management. The editor might send along a photographer to take some photographs of the children and a reporter to interview the proprietors and staff. All this publicity is *free*.

Leaflets and brochures

Design and print a quantity of leaflets informing parents of times and length of each session, number of places and ages of children catered for. Also include any special facilities such as music, computers or outdoor play, together with the number and level of trained staff employed and child to staff ratios. It is most important to include a telephone number and name where all interested parents can obtain more information at any time.

If you have a word processor or computer with a letter-quality printer, type in your material and print out as many copies as you require on your headed paper. If not, your choice may be between photocopies and printed leaflets. Printing 500 leaflets might just be better value than making photocopies at 10 pence a copy.

These leaflets could be posted through doors in the neighbourhood, placed in local shop windows, sub-post offices, libraries, doctors' surgeries, mother and baby clinics, toy shops, churches, adult education centres and recreational areas such as swimming pools. Fees and a detailed description of your playgroup or nursery can be included in a letter of introduction sent out as a follow-up to anybody interested by your leaflets. A small playgroup's sole source of publicity might be by leaflet.

If funds are available, it is wise to expand this idea into a brochure incorporating a couple of photos of the nursery and a comprehensive list of all the facilities available. A glossy brochure is important if you are running a day nursery, creche or workplace nursery and give a streamlined service and charge higher than average fees.

Your leaflet could also be sent to all the primary, prep and pre-prep schools in the vicinity. Some children from families with older brothers and sisters might enrol as a result.

An example of an introductory leaflet is shown on page 49. Many, of course, are much shorter, like the one on page 50.

The Apples Nursery School

Principals
Caroline Cox
Mrs. S. Goble

Hatt Common
Nr. Ball Hill
Newbury

The Apples Nursery School is situated in delightful countryside set well back from the road in its own grounds. The children have a spacious playground of an acre and their own flower bed for nature study.

We aim to provide a stimulating and caring environment catering for every child's needs. We gradually introduce phonetic and number work with games, rhymes and structured play, meanwhile developing motor skills until most children are capable of copying simple sentences by the time they leave us. Many children are also doing simple addition and subtraction before they go to school. Some children are ready for reading and more demanding work. We are there to guide and provide a learning environment.

We have fully qualified staff, with one teacher who specialises in nursery education, and nursery nurses. The team work together to provide a balanced, creative and learning atmosphere and are always available to answer any questions you may have.

We have a midmorning storytime with drama and singing and the children benefit from the musical talents of one of our nursery nurses. Cooking is a regular and much enjoyed activity and the children generally eat the results at break-time. Our afternoon children join us at 12 o'clock and we have a quiet time ensuring a gentle introduction to the afternoon activities and a calm end to the morning session. Children staying all day have a half-hour rest period after lunch. The lunch period is carefully supervised and the children enjoy their packed lunches.

In the afternoon we provide the same combination of introduction to basic motor skills combined with creative activities. The rising fives have an opportunity to consolidate their skills in preparation for school.

Please do not hesitate to contact us to arrange a visit as we are always delighted to show visitors around, this being the best way to see how we work.

The Apples Nursery	Highclere 253383
Morning session	9.00-12.30
Afternoon session	12.00-3.00
Full day	9.00-3.00

Caroline Cox	Home Number Newbury 42318
Mrs S. Goble	Home Number Newbury 32365

Specimen introductory leaflet

Are you looking for child care?
Have you considered registering your child with a day nursery?

______________________________ (Name)

______________________________ (Address)

is offering full day (8.00 am–5.45 pm)
or part-time facilities

The Nursery features:

- Bright, newly refurbished premises
- New equipment and toys
- Breakfast, lunch, tea and supper
- An educational programme

Phone ________________ (number) for our brochure.

Local authority lists

Telephone the Social Services Department of your local authority and ask the person in charge of playgroups and childminding for a list of child care services in your area. This person is usually called the under-fives officer, under-fives unit coordinator, pre-school adviser, or person in charge of day care for the under-fives. Your playgroup or nursery will automatically be included in this list once you have registered with the Social Services Department in your area. It will be placed in the private day care section. Since this list is sent out to those enquiring about private pre-school facilities, it is a good source of free publicity.

Yellow Pages

Place an advertisement in Yellow Pages for your nursery school, playgroup, creche or day nursery in the section headed Nurseries – child or Nursery schools.

Yellow Pages directories are compiled and published by British Telecommunications plc. Entries can be provided by contract (in the case of paid entries) or at the discretion of British Telecom (in the case of free entries for business subscribers). You are unlikely to qualify for a free advertisement. To place an advertisement dial 100 and ask for Freefone Telecom Business Sales.

A boxed ad will definitely catch the eye but this extra expense could be spared if your playgroup or nursery is the only one in the area. Choose a boxed ad if there are three or more.

Independent Schools Information Service (ISIS)

The Independent Schools Information Service (ISIS) publishes information on private, pre-prep and prep schools throughout the country. The London and South East region also publishes Under-Fives Sheets. Entry is by membership which costs £7.50 per year (1989-90). A nursery school can submit information, and it will be included in a list unless ISIS has received some negative feedback from questionnaires filled in by prep and pre-prep schools.

Registration form

A typical registration form is shown on page 52. Have this material typed on to a piece of your headed paper, then make as many photocopies as you require, or if you have a computer or word processor print out each form separately. A printed registration form is not necessary.

If children are registered for a creche or day nursery, the section on sessions can be deleted. Mention fees to parents when they telephone but do not include the amount in the leaflet or registration form.

A sudden increase in fees might be unavoidable. For instance, the church decides to increase your rent without much warning. There may be very little you can do if your nursery rents the best church hall in the region – or if all others are fully booked. Almost certainly, this increase will have to be passed on to the parents. If fees are printed on the leaflet or registration form, each time a similar occurrence happens you will have to have new forms.

It is a nice touch if you reply in writing to each enquiry. Fees can be stated in the letter. Tuck a leaflet inside this letter. This will take a little longer than sending out compliment slips but it is well worth it. An individual letter from a proprietor discussing their child will make parents look favourably on you and your nursery or playgroup.

Advertising

Advertising has to be paid for, so make sure that it is placed where parents likely to use your playgroup will see it; the local press (free and otherwise) is the obvious choice, as well as Yellow

REGISTRATION FORM

Please complete this form in capital letters and return it to the above address together with a cheque or postal order for £5 [exclude or change this amount if you wish]. This registration fee will be deducted from the first term's fees if your child decides to attend.

CHILD'S NAME ______________________________

(Forenames) (Surname)

DATE OF BIRTH ______________________ AGE ________

PARENT'S NAME ______________________________

AND ADDRESS ______________________________

____

____

____

HOME TEL NO ______________________________

WORK TEL NO ______________________________

WORKING HOURS ______________________________

* * *

EXPECTED DATE OF ENTRY ______________________

TICK SESSIONS REQUIRED

	MONDAY	TUESDAY	WEDNESDAY	THURSDAY	FRIDAY
AM	☐	☐	☐	☐	☐
PM	☐	☐	☐	☐	☐

* * *

CHILD'S DETAILS AND HISTORY

DOCTOR'S NAME ______________________________

AND ADDRESS ______________________________

____

____

TEL NO ______________________________

ALLERGIES (IF ANY) ______________________________

IMMUNISATIONS
(PLEASE TICK)

Has your child been immunised for any of the following?

Diphtheria	YES/NO	Tetanus	YES/NO
Whooping cough	YES/NO	Measles	YES/NO
Poliomyelitis	YES/NO	Measles, mumps, rubella	YES/NO

DATE BOOSTER IMMUNISATION RECEIVED ______________________

Has your child had any of the following childhood illnesses?

Measles	YES/NO	Chicken pox	YES/NO
Mumps	YES/NO	Whooping cough	YES/NO
Rubella	YES/NO		

* * *

ANYTHING ELSE WE SHOULD KNOW ______________________

FOOD DISLIKES OR INTOLERANCE ______________________

PARENT'S CONSENT FOR OUTINGS ______________________

Pages, but cards in shop windows might also be effective, as well as the parish magazine and local theatre programmes.

You can have a display or classified advertisement. A display ad needs to be designed, with a catchy headline, short text, and possibly a drawing or photograph; the leaflet on page 50 provides a starting point. Classified ads are typeset by the newspaper, but can stand out from the rest if there is space or a frame around them.

Classified ads are charged by the column centimetre, that is column width × depth in centimetres. Display ads are charged by fractions of a page, and you need to provide the necessary artwork. Make sure you get the artwork back for re-use in future.

Do not try to say too much, and make sure the reader is told how to follow up the advertisement. Give a name and phone number, and invite contact for more information.

A good signboard outside your nursery will attract attention from passers-by, so why not invest in one, making sure the size is within the local council's permitted limits?

Recommendations

Word of mouth recommendations are particularly useful to the survival of a nursery, playgroup or creche. Maintain a good relationship with parents old and new. Do not be opinionated. Always keep a low profile. If a child or a parent has a problem, it is likely that the parent will talk to you about it. A fee-paying child care facility can only run effectively and profitably if a good reputation is maintained. Parents can easily be scared away, especially those looking for a nursery for the first time, by a tenuous rumour that bears no relation to the truth. Therefore, always be discreet. If parents are pleased with the nursery school or playgroup their child attends, they will tell their friends and neighbours about it.

Open days, fêtes and bazaars

Once your playgroup or nursery is in operation, a series of open days can be planned so that parents hunting around for a playgroup or nursery can see how yours works. It is worth continuing with open days, even when all places are filled and you have a healthy waiting list, as they are a good advertisement. One never knows when competition might appear around the corner, and children tend to leave in clusters.

An open day, fête or bazaar is also one way of attracting the first intake of children. The nursery might not be completely finished but you have plans to open in two months' time so some form of open day is important. If the playgroup or nursery has a garden and it is summer, you could stage a summer fête with the future staff there to meet the parents. It might be better to let parents see a half-finished building but meet friendly, competent staff who can answer their questions, instead of waiting until the playgroup or nursery is ready to open and risk having a few places unfilled. On the whole, people are sympathetic. Even the Social Services Department of your local authority can be helpful. The present trend is to encourage the growth of nursery education and child care facilities in both the private and public sector.

Chapter 6

Equipment and Administration

Equipment

The major nursery equipment and toy suppliers who produce catalogues and offer a good mail order service are listed below. Their addresses are given in Chapter 14, unless they are likely to be in your local phone book.

- Community Playthings
- Nottingham Educational Supplies (NES)
- Galt
- Childsplay
- Hamleys
- Montessori Equipment Company
- Pre-school Playgroups Association (PPA) Promotion
- Offspring
- Philip & Tacey
- Edu-Play
- Escor Toys
- Caesarcraft
- Hestair Hope
- Playmatters
- Michael Stanfield
- Early Learning Centre
- Mothercare
- Habitat
- Boots
- Usborne

Write or telephone these companies for their catalogues. Any nursery school teaching the Montessori Method will want to order some Montessori equipment. This is available from the Montessori Equipment Company.

In addition to shopping by catalogue, it might be wise to look at shops in your area. Consult Yellow Pages for a list of shops in the toy and game shops category. There should also be sections headed toy and game manufacturers and toy and game wholesalers. Also look in the local press for forthcoming sales. You will be surprised how many things can be bought below list price. However, when weighing up prices take into account any discounts given by your regular suppliers. Some department stores now have sales twice a year and will often give a discount at other times of the year to regular customers. Do not be afraid to ask about discounts. You have the potential to be a good customer, so use it to your advantage.

Many towns have an Early Learning Centre where you can look

at the goods before you buy. Some large toy supermarkets also allow you to look at goods; for instance, Toys R Us. Sometimes it is possible to obtain a discount on the Fisher Price range of toys. Ask in your local toy shop. Members of the PPA receive a PPA Bonus Scheme enclosing vouchers for discounts on such things as Matchbox toys and Ladybird clothes, a few drinks and baby products. These amount to about £10 and can be looked at as a saving. In fact, the benefits of the PPA far outweigh the cost of membership, especially for a low-budget playgroup. (See Chapter 7 for details of membership.) Playmatters/The National Play Libraries Association also offers discounts to its members and gives advice on toys available throughout the country. Read *What Toy*, a consumer guide to toys and play.

Some local authorities can recommend suppliers in your area. Often the county council itself has equipment, such as tables and chairs, it wishes to dispose of. Look at any goods that are for sale. It is unlikely that a delivery service is available, so you will have to get any equipment bought back to your nursery or playgroup. Take into account any charges, such as van hire, when you are considering which supplier to use.

Several lists of equipment are given below. Prices have not been shown as they can decrease as well as increase at short notice, and because of the discounts available to some nurseries and playgroups. To decide on the supplier for each piece of equipment, choose the items you like then insert the price and supplier's name in the columns next to the item. Obtain three prices for each item of equipment. From this checklist and the funds available for equipment, pick which items can be bought and from whom. If equipment can be donated, place a tick in the donation column. Some lines are left free so that items of your own choice can be included. Do not write in this book but prepare your own list on A4 paper and make photocopies - you will almost certainly need more than one copy of each list.

If you wish to get an idea of prices, read the section on page 62 on how to set up for £500.

Essential equipment

Item	Supplier's names and prices			Donation
tables				
small chairs				
play mats				
beds or mattresses (if children stay all day)				

Item	Supplier's names and prices			Donation
cots (if babies attend all day)				
duvets/sheets (if children sleep at nursery)				
sleeping bags (if older children sleep at nursery)				
highchairs (if babies and toddlers attend all day)				
radio/cassette recorder				
television (not essential but useful)				
video (not essential but useful)				
plastic crates (for toy storage)				
baby change corner (if babies attend)				
double buggies (for day nursery only)				
painting easels/trays				
sand tray/sandpit (garden?)				
children's smocks				
children's mugs				
visitors' mugs				
plates				
cutlery				
cooker				
kettle				
fridge				
washing machine (if babies attend all day)				
lockable large storage cupboard				
shelves				
lockable desk and chair				
bookcase				
____________				
____________				
____________				
____________				
safety gates				
first aid tin				
first aid kit				

The purchase of the last three items is discussed in Chapter 8 on health and safety.

Administrative equipment

Item	Supplier's names and prices			Donation
lockable filing cabinet telephone answering machine typing machine word processor or microcomputer printer disks or typewriter ________ ________ ________ ________				

Again, cost these items. If you wish your business to be successful early on, most of this administrative equipment is essential. A professional approach means well-written, typed letters on a good quality machine. The new Amstrad word processor is good value. Locate one in your high street or shopping centre and familiarise yourself with the model. Sophisticated word processors and microcomputers that power letter-quality printers are available but unless you have free access to one (perhaps owned by somebody in your family), it is an unnecessary expense. Avoid second-hand machines.

An answering machine to take messages when the nursery or playgroup is closed is invaluable if the proprietors do not wish to give their home numbers to prospective parents. Many mail order companies advertising in the Sunday papers sell a combined telephone and answering machine for just over £100. If you buy a machine with a remote control facility, you can call the nursery or playgroup, for example, once an evening and at weekends, to play back the messages and return the urgent calls. If a parent has a problem on Friday evening, having to wait until Monday for an answer might be one reason to remove a child or look for an alternative facility.

If the nursery or playgroup is run in a private home, consider having another telephone line installed. This depends on the family involved. Some owners wish to work all the time during the start-up period; others do not wish to work after a certain time in the evening.

A photocopier is extremely useful. Desktop systems are now available from most office supplies outlets.

Large equipment

Large pieces of equipment, important for muscle development and hand/eye coordination, are listed below.

Item	Supplier's names and prices			Donation
climbing frame				
slide				
play house and contents				
bikes				
pushalongs				
children's buggies/prams				
__________				
__________				
__________				
__________				

Again, cost the items in this list in the same way as for essential equipment. Some may be expensive unless bought second-hand. Ask around schools and other playgroups in the neighbourhood for second-hand goods. Go to bring-and-buy sales and car boot sales. A charity shop can be a good inexpensive source of toys and books. If second-hand purchases are made, be sure to have items, such as a climbing frame, overhauled so that they are safe. Some nursery or playgroup proprietors find it cost-effective to employ a carpenter to custom-build and repair pieces of equipment.

Small equipment

If your initial funds are limited, essential pieces of equipment can be supplemented by small, less expensive items such as those listed overleaf.

Item	**Supplier's names and prices**			**Donation**
musical instruments				
jigsaws				
rolling pins and cutters				
round-tipped scissors				
dressing-up clothes				
books				
Duplo				
Lego				
Stickle Bricks				
shape sorters				
multi-cultural goods				
____________				
____________				
____________				
cars				
dolls				
pots and pans				
____________				
____________				
____________				

The larger pieces of equipment can be bought once the business shows a profit. Some groups raise funds for these items (see page 66) and aim to buy one large piece a year.

Consumables
Some consumables are listed below.

- paint
- crayons
- cardboard
- art paper
- paste
- playdough
- sugar paper

The quality and availability of consumables help to promote the image of a playgroup or nursery. This is especially important for a nursery school. The better the daily art and crafts project, the better the publicity. A child will always take his or her work home each week, or even at the end of each session. A drawing on good quality paper or a model will reinforce the parents' good opinion of the group. If the child goes home empty-handed, parents might think that nothing is happening at nursery school or playgroup. This is just as important for a playgroup where the emphasis is on play.

Allocate an amount to spend on consumables each term. The new proprietor may take a whole year to arrive at an amount for each term. An increase of, say, 10 per cent ought to be added to amounts each year to allow for inflation, etc. Consumables can be ordered once a term.

The consumables for use by the proprietors and helpers will include stationery such as envelopes, pens, pencils, paper clips, paper, index cards, stamps and files. Stationery for keeping accounts is given in Chapter 10.

Food and drink are consumed by helpers, children and parents in a nursery or playgroup. Since these supplies are usually bought weekly or daily, they warrant their own section (see page 64).

Loaned books, toys and tapes

The new group or low-budget playgroup can benefit from loaned books, toys and tapes. Obtain more information on how to participate from your local library. Most libraries will supply a box of library books each term. Some will deliver to the playgroup or nursery. The degree of local support will determine how many of these items need to be bought during the start-up period.

Receipt of goods

Ordered goods will nearly always arrive with a delivery note. Always check carefully the contents against the delivery note. The supplier should be notified immediately of any discrepancy. If it is obvious that the goods have been damaged during delivery or if one or more items are missing, it is better to refuse delivery and telephone the company immediately. If you notice that an item is damaged once you have unpacked the parcel, again notify the company concerned immediately. In both cases the company will give you instructions. Do not attempt to return any item until you have raised the query with the customer services department of the company supplying the goods. Be sure that your helpers are aware of these procedures so that they waste no time reporting any loss or damage.

Faulty goods and toys

Some goods will break soon after delivery. For instance, a pair of large cutting scissors can come out of alignment, making cutting awkward. Do not struggle on or try to repair the item yourself. Ring the manufacturer or catalogue company. Ask for its customer services department. Give the name of your playgroup or nursery, your account number and the invoice number of the order supplying the faulty goods. Explain the defect. Most companies will ask you to put this information in writing and return the defective item to them. In most cases you will be supplied with a new item as soon as possible.

How to set up for £500

If resources are limited, perhaps because the new proprietors are unwilling or unable to secure a bank loan and the facility planned is small (for example, they only have a licence for 12 children aged three to five years), a sum of £500 ought to be sufficient to establish a base of equipment.

For a playgroup in a private home, perhaps using the ground floor of the house with doors on to a garden or patio and taking eight to ten children, the biggest expense will be the purchase of essential equipment (and paying any staff).

Here is a breakdown of how £500 can be spent (1989/90):

	£
2 tables	99.90
10 small chairs	125.00
10 nursery beakers	9.90
10 nursery deep plates	22.50
10 pairs of round-tipped scissors	4.90
big card templates	5.95
square book rack	17.95
10 long-sleeved painting smocks	39.50
painting easel	29.95
Giant Duplo Basic Kit	59.95
4 multi-cultural books	21.00
truck	21.95
consumables	40.00

These prices were obtained from Nottingham Educational Supplies at the time of going to press. VAT is payable on some items. Children's clothes and books are exempt. It is wise to order from one supplier if possible, since a discount and free postage and packing may be included. Ring the company concerned before you place your order. Determine who is eligible for discount; for example, are PPA members given a discount? If no discount can be obtained, try another supplier. Having said this, Nottingham Educational Supplies who gave the above quote build all discounts into the catalogue price.

These items can be supplemented with donated toys and books and those bought second-hand with the few pounds spare. Some of the items could be bought second-hand, but do not give the impression to parents that everything has come from a jumble sale. A few brand new good quality games and toys are essential. For example, a long-sleeved painting smock for each child hanging on a peg looks professional. Likewise, attractive and unusual mugs and plates help to improve the image of the group. Read Chapter 9 for details of the kind of play and lessons that can be introduced.

Administration

The tasks of playgroup and nursery owners and helpers can be divided into the following categories:

- daily tasks for the care and education of the children given in the job description in Chapter 4
- food shopping
- cooking or supervising a cook
- making and serving snacks
- taking children to the loo or changing babies' nappies (some groups will not allow children to attend until they are out of nappies)
- answering the telephone
- making visiting parents feel welcome (see Chapter 5)
- checking each child is collected by the correct person (this is particularly important for one-off events where most parents or carers will not be known to the helpers; for example, at a creche held at a college of further education or at a shopping centre; each child and carer must be given the same coloured or numbered badge and only on presentation of that badge can the carer collect the child)
- cleaning the premises or supervising a cleaner
- ordering and maintaining equipment (see above)
- keeping an inventory of all equipment, using the costing sheets (see pages 56-60) together with the delivery notice and invoice for each piece of equipment to fill out an

equipment book or sheet (see Chapter 7)

- keeping an accident book (see Chapter 8)
- keeping accounts (see Chapter 10)
- paying rent (see Chapter 10)
- paying salaries, National Insurance and income tax (see Chapter 10)
- paying bills and keeping receipts (see Chapter 10)
- keeping and storing all receipts for cash purchases (see Chapter 10)
- keeping milk receipts and reclaiming the money once a quarter from the Department of Social Security (see page 65).

Cooking, food and drink

The level of the facility will determine how much food, if any, has to be prepared and cooked on site. A playgroup or nursery school in which those children who stay for lunch bring packed lunches will only be required to provide juice or milk at break times and a biscuit or a piece of fruit for each child. The proprietor could shop once a week or this could be one of the helper's responsibilities. Your milkman could deliver the milk and the juice. Encourage children to drink milk, since most of this expenditure can be reclaimed from the Department of Social Security. Some schools do not offer juice. The choice is between milk or water. Those children who are sensitive to cow's milk must not be given milk. When a child first starts in the group be sure that all helpers are aware of his or her allergies or food intolerance if any. This information can be obtained from the child's registration form or record card.

A creche or day nursery will almost certainly have to provide a hot lunch and often a high tea too. A well-equipped kitchen is therefore necessary. Funds must be put aside during the start-up period to fit and equip it. The kitchen should be carefully planned to include a large dishwasher, fridge, freezer, cooker and microwave; also a double sink, drainers, waste disposal and good work tops. All the necessary utensils are much the same as those for the home but it may be wise to buy caterers' sizes for such things as baking dishes, trays and saucepans. A large trolley will eliminate journeys from kitchen to dining room to serve food.

One or more cooks will be needed. There can be a balance between home-cooked food and frozen food. Finding the ideal balance is a matter of trial and error and this may take time to establish. Consider nutritional value, cost of ingredients, fuel costs, labour costs, shopping versus delivery and children's likes and dislikes. If your nursery relies heavily on frozen food, remember to take out adequate insurance cover so that damaged items can be replaced if a freezer cuts out. Each year increase the premium if necessary.

All kitchens should be locked when not in use. Children must never be allowed to enter the kitchen.

Free milk

Each child attending non-residential playgroup or nursery, creche or workplace nursery is entitled to one-third of a pint of milk free for each day he or she is present. To register for this benefit form WF/DN 15 can be obtained from the Director of Social Services of your local authority. Give details of the number of children attending each session, number of sessions per day (show only one session if the child attends all day), number of days open per week, date from which milk is to be supplied, together with the name and address of the registered premises. Return this completed form to the Director of Social Services of your local authority. It is also wise to include a letter explaining the situation. For example, if you have already bought milk for the children, explain the circumstances.

Apply for this benefit as soon as possible. Unfortunately, under Regulation 4 the Department of Social Security has no authority to reimburse playgroups or nurseries in respect of any period prior to their registration by the local Director of Social Services.

Once the Director of Social Services has signed the application it will be forwarded to the Department of Social Security for approval. Upon approval of your application you will be notified by letter, allocated a code number that should be quoted on all future correspondence, and supplied with a claim form WF/DN 16A for each quarter.

Completing form WF/DN16A

First read the information on the back of the form carefully. When filling in the actual numbers of children supplied with milk, place the numbers in the box for the correct day. These numbers will not always correspond with the attendance numbers, since some children may be intolerant to milk. You will be reimbursed for the actual price paid or for the price of ordinary milk, whichever is less.

It is also possible to claim for modified proprietory brands of baby milk for children under one and for children's vitamin drops.

Remember to keep all the milk receipts together and have a separate entry in the petty cash book for milk. Enclose the milk receipts (or photocopies of the relevant pages in the petty cash book if you have no receipts) with your application. Send off your application promptly at the end of the three-month period.

Fund raising

Some independent groups never consider fund raising. They feel that parents pay fees and should not be approached for additional contributions. Since few grants are available to privately funded groups, the sole source of revenue may be fees. Fund raising can be one way of speeding up the purchase of a large piece of equipment; for example, a climbing frame for muscle development, a photocopier for making stencils and home-made books or a video recorder for running educational videos. Judge the situation carefully before embarking on a fund-raising drive.

You could begin by getting a T-shirt and a sweatshirt printed with your playgroup or nursery's logo. Offer these for sale to parents. If the response is good, get more shirts printed. A uniform seems a little silly for the under-fives but some parents might like to send their children wearing the school's colours. This is also good advertising, especially in summer when the children are not wearing coats and everybody can see the logo.

Put the profits into a bank account opened for the specific item. Then develop this into a fund-raising scheme of picnics, open days, sales, children's shows, etc. Any surplus could be spent on an outing. If staged correctly, a small fund-raising drive each year can benefit children, parents and the group.

Catalogue shopping is another way of raising money for the group and offering a saving to parents. A table with catalogues (be sure that these companies offer discounts) could be placed near the door at delivery and collection times. Parents can choose the toys or books they wish to order and place the name of the item and its amount on a ruled sheet. At the end of the week, or time allocated, make out the order. Divide the discount evenly between the school and the parent and charge each parent the correct amount. Collect all cheques or cash before you place the orders. The parents should be pleased to receive a small discount and the group can increase its funds. This might be well received during the autumn term when parents are thinking about Christmas presents. A Giant Duplo Basic Set costs £61.95 (1989/90) plus VAT from Galt. However, Galt offers a discount of 5 per cent to PPA members - this means a saving of a couple of pounds to the parent and the same amount for the nursery or playgroup. Usborne will supply a free book each time an order of a certain size is filled. Their list includes several well-planned and illustrated books, such as *Letters, Numbers and Colours: The Alphabet, Counting and Colours for Beginners*, which are less than £5.

The message is: be flexible. Each year the mix of parents changes as some children leave to take up primary education. One year nearly every family might be enthusiastic about fund-raising events, perhaps because there is a high percentage of non-working mothers. Another year there may be very little interest. Often parents are generous if fund-raising events are infrequent and evently spaced throughout the school year.

Events

Supply all stall holders, etc at any fund-raising event or sale with enough petty cash bags. All change must be bagged up properly. If this is left to one person at the end, it can take a long time. This is annoying if you want to lock up in a hurry, for instance. Get the money ready. Make the entries in the appropriate paying-in book(s). Take the funds to the bank as soon as possible. When the function is held in the evening you might have to keep the cash until the bank opens. Look at your insurance policy to be sure that this money is insured against theft and all risks while in transit. Ask at your branch if there are any arrangements for depositing cash in a night safe deposit box.

Chapter 7

Insurance

Good insurance cover is a priority for any playgroup or nursery. This is important for those groups offering part-time care as well as for those that take responsibility for their charges for the entire day. A child climbing a tree or playing on the stage of a church hall could fall and be concussed. A fight between two children could result in an eye injury. With a good health and safety campaign and adequate supervision these calamities can be avoided. But the playgroup or nursery must have sufficient cover to settle any claims made by the parents if there is a calamity. Insufficient cover could result in a loss of livelihood, a bankrupt business and even the loss of a proprietor's home.

Insurance is high on the list of things to organise. Do not wait until your playgroup or nursery is registered. Burglary can happen at any time. This may even be more likely when premises are being used infrequently. A playleader might hurt her back when setting up equipment before playgroup opens!

The amount of cover is the amount of money an insurance company will pay out when a claim is made. The premium is the amount the policy holder pays for a particular policy. Do not underinsure your business. Premiums may be high but they are considered a deductible expense by the Inland Revenue.

The different types of insurance policy available are given below. How to make a claim and how to maintain an up-to-date inventory of equipment are also explained. A few child care associations offer package policies which can be taken out only with membership, so the second part of this chapter describes the organisations that can help proprietors setting up and running a child care business. Annual membership dues, benefits and insurance policies, if any, are given.

Types of insurance

Insurance can be obtained through a child care association, an insurance broker, accountant or solicitor. Three organisations to contact for help are the British Insurance Brokers' Association, FIMBRA and the Association of British Insurers.

The type of child care facility usually determines the level of insurance required. A playgroup registered for 12 children for five mornings a week may find that the PPA group insurance underwritten by Sun Alliance and London Insurance plc is sufficient and inexpensive (see page 78). A day nursery whose employees have sole responsibility for the care of 24 children for eight hours a day would require more extensive (and expensive) cover, and this ought to be bought with the help of a well-known insurance broker. Be sure the broker is registered with the Insurance Brokers' Council. The British Insurance Brokers' Association will be able to tell you of brokers on this list. If you know an accountant or solicitor, or have a good working relationship with your bank manager, ask for advice.

Always obtain three quotes from which to choose the one that best suits the needs of your nursery. Read each prospectus carefully. When you are satisfied with the policy and have chosen the amount of cover, fill in a proposal form - another name for an application form. Return this with a cheque for the correct amount before the first intake of children arrives. An insurance cover note will be issued by the insurers. There might be a short delay but cover is often effective from the date the cheque is received. The cover note gives details of the type of cover obtained, the policy number, the premiums received, the equipment sum insured, the date cover terminates and any other details, such as additional cover for a parent and toddler group, personal insurance or buildings insurance.

Most large companies take payment by direct debit instalments. You are required to complete a direct debit form giving the name, address and sorting code of your bank, and the name and account number of your nursery. You must also sign a Credit Agreement regulated by the Consumer Credit Act 1974 which will be sent to you. This will run until a written notice of cancellation is sent or all the premiums have been collected for the year. A sheet with the right to cancel should be sent to you each year. If the insurance is kept up over subsequent years, new forms will have to be completed and signed each year.

Instalments are charged to your account on a fixed day each month for the required number of months. General Accident, for instance, collects over a period of five months. There may be a small charge for this service. If this is more than a few pounds, consider paying by cheque in one instalment.

Policies sold by individual insurers can differ in the cover they provide and in their terms and conditions. Some playgroups will not require all these levels of insurance. A small playgroup that rents a church hall will not require buildings insurance. This is almost certainly the responsibility of the church. If you do rent, get your lease looked at by the underwriters before completing the proposal form. Premiums increase most years, so build this into your budget.

Established in 1985 the Association of British Insurers represents over 430 insurance companies which form a substantial part of the British insurance market. It publishes many useful leaflets on every type of insurance. Telephone or write to the association for a comprehensive list of its publications. This includes a set of small business insurance advice files. Many can be obtained free of charge by sending a stamped and addressed envelope.

Employers' liability

Employers' liability insurance is required by law if a playgroup or nursery employs helpers. This allows damages to be paid to one or more employees if injured or ill as a result of working in the playgroup or nursery. The amount of cover is often unlimited.

Upon receipt of the annual premium, a Certificate of Employers' Liability Insurance is issued bearing a policy number and date of commencement and expiry of insurance. This certificate must be pinned on to the playgroup's or nursery's noticeboard. If employees from more than one nursery are covered by the same insurance policy, photocopies of the certificate must be displayed at each place of business. The insurance is usually valid from the date the premiums were received. Check with your insurance broker or the association or intermediary selling the policy that this is correct.

Public liability

Public liability covers the proprietor's liability for injury, illness or death caused to members of the general public including the children attending the playgroup or nursery or their parents, or accidental damage to their property as a result of the activities of the playgroup or nursery. A limit of indemnity of £1 million or more for any one occurrence plus legal expenses is advisable. Accidents as a result of outings, fêtes, summer fairs, jumble sales, and the use of a public swimming pool or park, for example, are covered. This is essential.

Equipment

Personal effects and the group's equipment and contents can be insured against fire and theft. Other risks such as aircraft, explosion, riot and civil commotion, malicious acts, impact by road vehicles, storm, flood and escape of water from tanks or pipes can also be insured against. It is important that the playgroup or nursery's equipment is adequately insured while on the premises or in transit. Since replacing toys and large pieces of equipment can be expensive, the standard cover is very often for £2000–£3000. This cover can be increased if an additional premium is paid. An up-to-date inventory of equipment (see page 75) ought to enable you to put a price on the value of the equipment. Do not forget to add in the current retail price for each item of donated or second-hand equipment. Some policies replace equipment on a new for old basis so that the full retail cost of a damaged or lost item is refunded regardless of its original condition. Personal effects are usually insured for far less.

A business interruption insurance to protect against loss of fees due to children not being able to attend, because the premises have been damaged by fire or flood for instance, is a necessary addition (see the section on loss of income on page 72).

Frozen food

Frozen food cover against damage to food in freezers caused by breakdown or power failure is important for a day nursery or creche that serves cooked meals and relies on some frozen meals and main ingredients.

Contingency liability

This covers the use of cars by employees, helpers and proprietors on playgroup or nursery business if they have an accident. It does not replace third-party or comprehensive motor insurance and is not valid if the vehicle in question is uninsured. Remember, it is an offence to allow others to drive your car without insurance. State clearly on the proposal form the conditions under which vehicles are used for playgroup or nursery business. If the proprietors' cars are driven by helpers, for example to do shopping, take out an all drivers policy. This policy might not be necessary for those living in cities where public transport is good, but some package policies include contingent motor liability free of charge.

Loss of money

The term 'money' includes cash, cheques, stamps, postal orders and money orders. Playgroup or nursery funds in addition to the personal money of employees, helpers and proprietors ought to be insured against loss and theft from the premises or in transit. Never leave money unattended, though. The cover for any one loss could be fixed at £250 for playgroup or nursery funds and £50 for personal money. This cover is necessary even if all fees are paid by cheque.

This policy, however, does not give protection against money stolen by an employee. A fidelity guarantee insurance policy will provide cover for this.

Personal accident

This covers accidental injury of proprietors, employees, helpers, children registered with the playgroup or nursery and helpers' children. Benefits include a pay-out on death or permanent disablement. This insurance is recommended, but get advice on how much cover is required.

Buildings insurance

Buildings insurance covers the actual building that houses the playgroup or nursery against fire, storm, flood and certain other disasters. If the playgroup is held in a proprietor's home, it may be possible to pay an additional premium to extend the insurance policy already taken out on the building. Again, do not underinsure the property. Insure for the full rebuilding costs, professional fees and site clearance. To arrive at the rebuilding costs, multiply the rebuilding costs per square foot by the number of square feet of the playgroup or nursery. Consult the Association of British Insurers, your local business association or club, and several builders in your area so that the per square foot rebuilding costs are correct for your region. Be sure that the cost of rebuilding materials and labour is updated each year and an additional premium is paid if necessary. Don't forget to allow a sum to replace fixtures and fittings.

Loss of income

A business interruption policy compensates for loss of profits caused by insured events as well as the increased costs incurred as a result. Think about damaging events, estimate the length of time needed to get the business going again, and fix a sum accordingly.

This could protect against loss of fees because the children are unable to attend due to the premises being damaged by fire, flood or some other peril. This is necessary if the playgroup or nursery is large and will not transfer easily to a proprietor's home. The cover will pay the salaries of employees and helpers, and the proprietors if they receive a wage, and any rent on temporary accommodation. It will also maintain profits if the playgroup or nursery is making a profit.

Key person insurance

Since most playgroup or nursery proprietors work with the children in their playgroup or nursery, this cover is essential. Some groups are entirely dependent upon their owners, employing no other helpers. An amount of £250,000, for instance, could be paid to the policy holder in the event of the death of one or other of the partners. It is important that sufficient funds can be generated at this time, since the remaining partner might well have to buy out the other partner's share of the business.

Personal insurance

The proprietors and their families must first be adequately insured. This is important when starting a new business and it may be conditional upon taking out a business loan as well as business insurance.

Read Chapter 10 if you are considering a pension scheme, permanent health insurance or life assurance.

Credit insurance

This provides cover against the risks of debtors becoming insolvent and unable to pay. This is unnecessary for a playgroup or nursery, since the only debtors could be parents. If parents fall behind with the payment of their fees, the proprietors should ask them not to send their children to playgroup or nursery again and to pay up. Any amount not paid within a specified period could be reclaimed through the county court.

If you are running a large workplace nursery, however, and have several large companies as clients who settle their employees' accounts, it might be worth looking into this kind of policy. A large organisation filling five places in a private day nursery with its employees' children might make this cover worthwhile in the event of the organisation collapsing.

Change of premises

If the underwriters are informed of a change of premises, the cover will usually be transferred automatically. This might be a more frequent occurrence in the rented sector; for example, a church hall can be sold for redevelopment or may be requisitioned for the sole use of the church.

Once a change of address is being considered, write to the company that has underwritten the policy, your insurance broker or the intermediary that supplied the group's insurance, to clarify the situation. For instance, if your playgroup or nursery is moving to an area that is considered to be more at risk from theft, premiums might be increased. This could also be the case if the group relocates to the centre of a major city.

How to make a claim

First check your policy to make sure that the type of damage you are claiming for is covered. Theft of, or damage to, property can be a more frequent occurrence than disablement, death or fire. Therefore, how to make a claim for loss or damage to the group's equipment or a helper's property is taken as an example. Some policies may ask for different information. First telephone your insurance company asking for a claim form. It will send you a theft and all risks claim form.

A claim for theft can be considered only if the robbery is reported to the police as soon as it is discovered. The police station will issue a crime reference number. This must be inserted on the claim form. Make your claim as soon after the incident as possible.

Note that a playgroup or nursery cannot recover VAT paid on new equipment. Once registered under the Nurseries and Child-minders Regulation Act 1948, as amended by the Health Services and Public Health Act 1968, a playgroup or nursery is exempt from VAT. Therefore, it is unlikely that a playgroup or nursery will register for VAT, so tick the box wholly exempt. Many theft and all risks policies now pay out on a new for old basis, so a deduction for wear and tear or for salvage value is not always required. Most claims should be substantiated with at least one builder's estimate for rebuilding work and receipts for sale or purchase for any items lost or damaged. Send photocopies and not the originals but do check with your insurance company that these are acceptable. If you are asked to send originals, be sure to photocopy them first.

Return the completed claim form to the address indicated accompanied by a letter quoting your policy number and the date the incident occurred. If your claim is rejected and you think the insurers should have paid out, the Association of British Insurers' consumer department or nearest regional office may be able to help, if your insurers are a member of the Association.

Inventory of equipment

For insurance purposes, and for the playgroup or nursery's own records, it is important that an inventory of equipment is compiled. If you use a word processor or microcomputer with a letter-quality printer, set up an inventory file. Divide the page into five columns. The first column lists the name of the item purchased with the name of the supplier placed below in parentheses. The second, third and fourth columns show the date of order, delivery and payment respectively. The last column indicates the amount spent with the number of the cheque placed below in parentheses. Be sure to enter each item as it is ordered, delivered and purchased. An example of an inventory of equipment purchased by a small playgroup during its first year is given below. When making a claim or updating insurance cover each year, add in the price of a new item for each of the second-hand items denoted by an asterisk. Do a spot check on some of the other items, comparing the original price with the current price. If prices have risen noticeably since the previous year, add in a figure in line with inflation. Reprice all your equipment once every three to four years. During periods of high inflation adjust figures annually.

Those proprietors who do not use a computerised system can set up their inventory in a large hard-backed ruled book. If one entry is allowed to run over two facing pages, there will be sufficient room for three or four extra columns at the far right-hand side. The inflation-proof prices for subsequent years can be placed in these columns.

Set up a similar table listing all other contents of your playgroup or nursery. Call it general inventory.

Keep two copies of each inventory. Store one on the premises together with your insurance policy and the other at the home of one of the proprietors. This will safeguard against losing all records in a fire or flood.

Inventory of equipment

Piece of equipment (Supplier)	Date			Amount (Cheque number)
	Ordered	Delivered	Invoice paid (Invoice number)	
slide* (Speak)	23/6/87	23/6/87	23/6/87	£ 15.00 (100003)
4 tables* (Greater London Supplies)	23/7/87	23/7/87	23/7/87	£ 8.00 (100007)

Piece of equipment (Supplier)	Date			Amount (Cheque number)
	Ordered	Delivered	Invoice paid (Invoice number)	
climbing frame (Community Playthings)	28/9/87	29/9/87	8/10/87	£371.68 (100016)
small equipment, mugs, etc (NES)	12/10/87	15/10/87	6/11/87	£ 74.55 (100021)
multi-cultural, puppets, Playmobile people (Galt)	15/10/87	21/10/87	4/12/87	£ 88.26 (100030)
painting smocks (Greater London Supplies)	15/10/87	22/10/87	4/1/88	£ 36.00 (100031)
Duplo (Greater London Supplies)	15/10/87	15/10/87	4/1/88	£149.08 (100031)
brushes (Greater London Supplies)	12/11/87	12/11/87	4/1/88	£ 1.80 (100031)
jigsaws* (parents)	12/11/87	12/11/87	12/11/87	£ 8.00 (cash)
doll's pushchair, teaset (toy fair)	16/2/88	16/2/88	16/2/88	£ 18.97 (100040)
boxes (market)	16/3/88	16/3/88	16/3/88	£ 50.00 (100043)
boxes (market)	27/4/88	27/4/88	27/4/88	£ 13.38 (100049)
dressing up (Galt)	18/3/88	10/4/88	6/5/88	£ 50.27 (100051)
dressing up, mats (NES)	18/3/88	10/4/88	6/5/88	£ 63.83 (100052)
dressing up, puppets (NES)	1/5/88	11/5/88	11/6/88	£ 35.90 (100071)
puzzles (Childsplay)	4/88	11/5/88	11/6/88	£ 25.22 (100070)
mats for climbing frame (Community Playthings)	20/5/88	25/5/88	25/6/88	£345.00 (100069)
trikes (tiny × 2) play tunnel (Galt)	20/5/88	31/5/88	30/7/88	£ 82.05 (100080)

* = second-hand purchase

Child care associations

Pre-school Playgroups Association (PPA)

The Pre-school Playgroups Association (PPA) was founded in

1960 by a group of parents with young children. It is a democratic voluntary organisation funded by central government and some charities. The branches fall into ten regions. Each branch has its own committee of volunteers which organises training courses for parents and playleaders and administers any grant money. The degree of support varies from region to region, so telephone your regional office to find out the resources available in your area. Grant money is not given to privately funded groups but your local branch could help on other issues. The PPA has a team of fieldworkers who work from home, in addition to training and development officers and national advisers.

Besides funding PPA voluntary playgroups and parent and toddler groups, it also gives advice to its members who run playgroups in the private sector.

It publishes a wide range of literature. Most are free leaflets and others are very cheap. The PPA National Centre will supply members with a publications list and free leaflets.

Group membership

There are two kinds of group membership, standard and open. Open membership applies to those setting up or running profit-making groups. Annual membership is £31 (1989/90). This subscription includes:

- ten issues a year of the PPA's house magazine *Contact* which presents features, ideas, letters, bookshelf and news from PPA groups
- six issues of *Under Five*
- PPA Bonus Scheme
- membership pack containing a membership card, information sheets, a poster and a resource list
- PPA publications
- discount on PPA goods and gifts
- inexpensive insurance
- a right to vote at the national AGM
- support from your branch

From the list of branches supplied with your membership determine your branch code and remember to give this code together with your membership number whenever you write to, or speak to, PPA regional offices or its National Centre.

Insurance

Only current group members may take out PPA insurance. The cover is good. No individual policies are issued. All members wishing to purchase insurance do so as part of the master policy held at the PPA National Centre. The PPA group insurers is the Sun Alliance and London Insurance plc. To obtain a prospectus and to be sure that your group falls within the PPA's definition of a playgroup, parent and toddler group, under-fives group or day care group write to, or telephone, the PPA National Centre. If you are not yet a group member ask for membership details too. The proposal form and the membership form are on one sheet. Your insurance will be effective from the time your payment is received by the PPA. An acknowledgement of this can be obtained if you send a stamped addressed envelope with your remittance. You will receive a cover note in due course.

There are two types of cover. A premium of £19.25 (1989/90) secures cover type B; equipment is insured at £2500. A premium of £16.50 (1989/90) secures cover type A; equipment is insured at £1500. An additional £500-worth of equipment cover costs only £1 (1989/90). All equipment claims are processed on a new for old basis. Besides cover for equipment, employers' liability, public liability, contingent motor liability, loss of money and personal accident are all included for the same premium. Cover for the other categories mentioned in this chapter can be taken out by special arrangement. Type C cover is available for day care groups.

Insurance and membership renewal forms are sent out in February each year. The insurance year runs from 1 April to 31 March. For each year of membership be sure to complete every shaded area on the form, check your address and post code are correct, allow at least one month for the form to be processed, and fill in your cheque payable to PPA.

Montessori Association of Teachers and Schools (MATS)

The Association, formerly the London Montessori Centre International Association, was formed to help all Montessori students and schools, providing communication between its members, and discounts and special rates where possible. Membership is open to schools (£50) and teachers (£20). Each must also pay a registration fee of £30. The above rates apply for 1989/90.

A school member can benefit from:

- a subscription to its house journal, *Montessori Courier*, published bi-monthly

- registration and privileges with the Montessori Teachers and Nannies' Job Agency
- 5 per cent discount on workshop registration
- first offer of restricted places on Saturday seminars
- 5 per cent off all purchases of Montessori apparatus.

MATS-accredited Montessori schools can make use of the Youth Training Scheme to provide on-the-job training of suitable school-leavers and young Montessori trainees, supplemented by formal correspondence and workshop training.

Teacher members enjoy fewer privileges, but being a member of this Association can only benefit a Montessori nursery school, or teacher.

Other bodies and associations

Other organisations such as the National Childminding Association, National Children's Bureau, Workplace Nurseries, Professional Association of Nursery Nurses (PANN), Gingerbread and Playmatters/The National Toy Libraries Association can help those working in or running a child care business. Their addresses and telephone numbers are given in Chapter 14.

Chapter 8

Health and Safety

A good health and safety campaign is of the utmost importance. Parents want the assurance that their child is safe when in the care of a playgroup or nursery. The Social Services Department gives top priority to safety too. Helpers *must* know what to do if there is a fire, an accident, or if something untowards happens on an outing.

Immunisation

Be sure that each child's registration form has been completed before the child is given a place. Any vaccines or childhood illnesses that the child has had must be included. The common vaccines are:

1. triple injection against diphtheria, tetanus and whooping cough administered as three doses: the first at three months, the second six to eight weeks after the first, and the third six months after the second;
2. polio vaccine given by mouth at the same time intervals as the triple injection;
3. MMR for measles, mumps and rubella given by injection at 14 months.

A booster injection of diphtheria and tetanus vaccine and an oral dose of polio vaccine are usually given before the child goes to school at five. However, children over three years old attending full-time nursery or creche should be taken to their doctor or clinic so that this can be done earlier.

In Britain all children are routinely offered immunisation against the childhood illnesses listed opposite. Unfortunately, the uptake in Britain is far lower than the World Health Organisation's target uptake for immunisation of 95 per cent by 1995. All those in the child care network could help reach this goal by educating parents. The contraindications to immunisation are rare. Parents are only asked to have a supply of paracetamol to give the child after immunisation if he or she

Quick guide to infectious diseases

Illness and incubation period (days)	Symptoms	Period when infectious	Minimum period of exclusion
chickenpox 11-21	cold, red spots turn into blisters, and dry up	1 day before to 6 days after appearance of rash	6 days from onset of rash
rubella or German measles 14-21	cold, swollen glands, pin head rash	few days before to 4 days after onset of rash	4 days from onset of rash (avoid women who are less than 14 weeks pregnant)
measles 10-15 (commonly 10 to onset of symptoms 14 to appearance of rash)	cold, runny nose, pinkish eyes, dry cough, spots on neck and face	few days before to 5 days after onset of rash	7 days from onset of rash
mumps 12-26 (commonly 18)	1-2 days' fever, loss of appetite, headache and swelling on both sides of jaw	few days before to subsidence of swelling	until swelling has gone
whooping cough or pertussis 7-10	varied, mild cough and cold for 10 days, spasms of coughing ending in vomiting, cough lasts for several weeks	from 7 days after exposure to 21 days after onset of paroxysmal cough	21 days from onset of paroxysmal cough

The exclusion period for skin infections is until treament has been received for cases of pediculosis and scabies and until the spots have healed in cases of impetigo.

These guidelines are laid down by the Department of Education and Science and the Department of Health for the control of infectious diseases in schools.

develops a fever. Doctors recommend that even children with stable neurological conditions such as cerebral palsy be immunised.

Reaction to milk, eggs, wheat or fish

If a child has a reaction to milk, eggs, wheat or fish, this should be clearly indicated on the child's registration form and the child should not be given the offending food. Fifty to a hundred people out of 10,000 cannot tolerate cow's milk, either the lactose content, the protein or both. Soya milk, goat's milk and sheep's milk are alternatives. However, some children may have a reaction to these products, so watch the child carefully. The best step may be to eliminate milk altogether. Work with the parents especially if the child has most meals at your nursery or creche. Wyeth Laboratories, a manufacturer of soya milk, has produced the *Wysoy Mixed Feeding Guide* that includes some milk-free and egg-free dishes and Diana Wells, a state registered nurse and sick children's nurse, has published a booklet called *What Can I Give Him Today?: 50 Milk, Egg and Additive Free Recipes* available from Hanbury Guest House for a small charge.

If a child has a reaction to wheat, give gluten-free products only. Most are marked by the symbol of an ear of corn.

Allergies

With allergies you must work with the parents concerned.

Balanced diet

A balanced diet is essential to a growing child above six months of age. Babies under six months can get all their daily requirements from milk even if solids are not introduced.

The diet must include sufficient fats, proteins, minerals and vitamins, and contain enough calories to support growth and play. A balanced diet contains some animal products such as milk, eggs, fish and meat, some fresh vegetables and fruit, and enough cereal and bread or potatoes to provide energy.

There are four categories of vitamin. These are

Vitamin	Found in	Needed for
A	egg yolk, milk fat, green and yellow vegetables	normal growth and development of skin, eyes, intestinal and bronchial linings
B	whole grains, milk, eggs, liver, meat, green vegetables, fruit and yeast	vital for growth and normal body function

Vitamin	Found in	Needed for
C	citrus fruits, tomatoes, potatoes (easily destroyed by cooking)	development and maintenance of body's supporting structure
D	margarine but few other foods	growth of teeth and bones and helps absorption of calcium from food

It is important that children under five get sufficient calcium and vitamin D. A good diet is better than a poorer diet supplemented with vitamin drops. Note that some vitamin supplements contain lactose.

Food storage and cooking

Most cases of food poisoning can be avoided by proper cooking procedures. Some bacteria produce a toxin in food even if food is heated or treated and this toxin is likely to cause illness. Others such as *Salmonella* do not produce toxin. They can be killed and are safe if food is cooked properly.

Storage of food is as important as proper cooking. All refrigerators should operate at a temperature of 5°C (41°F) or lower. Freezers should operate at a temperature of -15°C (5°F). Keep a thermometer in each compartment and have all appliances overhauled regularly.

If there is a power cut for three hours or longer, examine the contents of the freezer and check that each item is still frozen. This is more likely in a well-stocked freezer. Use any thawed food immediately. Only cook food from frozen if recommended to do so by the manufacturer.

Always wash your hands after handling raw meat or poultry. Pack your refrigerator carefully: cooked food at the top, raw food at the bottom, and raw poultry, meat and fish at the very bottom.

Food additives and E numbers

Additives are used as preservatives, colouring, emulsifiers, stabilisers, thickeners, flavouring, antioxidant and processing aids. The Food Labelling Regulations state that all additives in food should be identified by category or function and name or serial number on the packaging. Many serial numbers are preceded by E which means that the additive has been presumed safe for use in food in EC countries. Unfortunately, flavouring need only be described by the word flavouring.

The Ministry of Agriculture, Fisheries and Food produces a book entitled *Food Additives, The Numbers Identified* which lists all permitted additives by name and serial number. Most supermarkets will tell you of their range of preservative-free and colour-free food if you write to their customer services department. *The Additive Checklist: A Shopper's Guide to the Additives in Food Produced by Leading Manufacturers and Supermarkets* by S Lashford is published by Ashgrove Press; *The New E for Additives* by M Hanssen and J Marsden is published by Thorsons.

Many additives are naturally occurring compounds extracted from other food. Vitamins and minerals are not additives.

Give the children a varied diet. Small qualities of almost anything are unlikely to be harmful. However, if you wish to know more, subscribe to *The Food Magazine* available from the London Food Commission. The London Food Commission also publishes books on additives, healthy eating, school meals, and food and drink for the under-fives. Its education and training programme provides one-day courses which may be of interest to nursery nurses and others working in playgroups and nurseries. Send a stamped addressed envelope for a brochure and publications list.

Windows

Never leave windows accessible to toddlers and young children open and unfastened. Apply childproof locks even if your playgroup or nursery is on the ground floor. There are different types of lock available for sash windows, wood hinged windows and metal hinged windows. To buy and fit locks for eight windows can cost less than £100. Locks will also help to prevent burglary.

Patio doors and french windows, perhaps on to an outside play area, should be fitted with locks top and bottom. If they house glass panels, have safety glass fitted or cover each pane with adhesive safety film to prevent ordinary glass from shattering. Teach children to play away from glass doors and low windows.

Doors

All doors should be fitted with deadlocks that can only be opened with a key. For additional security fit a five-lever mortise deadlock which conforms with British Standards BS3621. A door chain and spy hole on the main door may be advisable in built-up areas. Install door hinge bolts and security bolts to lessen the chances of burglary. Consult the police crime prevention officer and your insurers. If you are buying an existing business or using existing premises, change all locks. An alarm system may not be necessary; crime prevention is a better approach.

The main door should be manned at all times when the children are entering or leaving playgroup or nursery. A system of double doors enclosing a small vestibule may help to ensure that no children escape and that each is collected by parents or persons authorised to do so.

Electricity supply

Electrical points should be self-shutting or, better still, should be inaccessible. Perhaps you only need a power supply in the kitchen. Always lock the kitchen except when a member of staff is there. Never let children into the kitchen.

Tape all plugs to exposed sockets; for example, those to a television and a video recorder. Alternatively, when the nursery is being adapted for use ask the electrician to place all plugs in the classroom about six feet from the ground. This may, however, inconvenience helpers who are small in stature.

Fit all electrical appliances with short curly flexes, especially kettles. Avoid extension cords and adaptors. Replace all frayed or damaged flexes. Overhaul and replace faulty equipment if necessary. Call a qualified electrician. Surround each radiator or portable heater with a large guard. Avoid paraffin heaters.

Gas supply

Install safe gas taps. All gas appliances should be installed by a member of British Gas or CORGI. Have all appliances serviced regularly, especially central heating systems. Get work done when the children are on holiday or over a weekend.

Cot safety

Those nurseries and creches that take babies will need to buy cots. Check that all cot sides are firm and the spacing between the bars is narrow. Use a safety mattress but no pillow. Place babies where they can be heard and have company. Cot safety catches will be needed once the child reaches five months. The British Standards Institution has published the *BSI Nursery and Child Safety Products Register* available for an annual subscription.

Stairs

Check all wooden stairs and floors for splinters. Block all stairs with safety gates that conform to British Standards.

Fire prevention

Each playgroup or nursery will be inspected by the Fire Service before its registration is approved by the Social Services Department. The fire officer will explain fire exits, signs and procedures to you.

Once your playgroup or nursery is up and running, have regular fire drills prompted by a fire bell used solely for this purpose. Are the drill procedures the same for a flood alert?

Hang a fire blanket on the wall behind the cooker. Install fire extinguishers and smoke detectors. Ensure they are properly maintained. Keep windows and doors in good repair. Make fences and gates high enough to keep children in and burglars or arsonists out.

Road safety

Teach children the colour and order of traffic lights, how to use a pelican crossing and the major points given in the Green Cross Code. Pedestrians should always give drivers time to stop at crossings. The Tufty Club for under-sevens encourages children to act safely. *Crossing Roads* by Althea published by Dinosaur Books/RoSPA explains road safety clearly to the under-fives.

Be particularly aware of safety if taking children out of the playgroup or nursery. Supervision must be good, parents' consent given, carry the first aid box with you, and take a list of important telephone numbers for each child who attends.

First aid box

A first aid box (recommended by the Health and Safety Executive) for a playgroup or nursery staffed by ten helpers or less contains:

- 1 guidance card
- 20 individually wrapped sterile adhesive dressings
- 2 sterile eye pads with attachment
- 2 triangular bandages
- 2 sterile coverings for serious wounds (where applicable)
- 6 safety pins
- 6 medium-sized sterile unmedicated dressings
- 2 large sterile unmedicated dressings
- 2 extra large sterile unmedicated dressings
- pair of sharp scissors
- pair of tweezers
- roll of non-allergic adhesive tape (micropore)
- packs of sterile gauze
- crepe bandages
- first aid box (tin, plastic or wood, not cardboard) marked with a white cross on a green background

First aid courses

The Pre-school Playgroups Association (PPA) and St John Ambulance organise first aid courses at adult education centres. Certificates such as the Adult First Aid Certificate as authorised by St John Ambulance are awarded. There may be a charge but this usually includes registration, manual, and course and examination fees. A course usually runs for six to eight weeks. There should be at least two trained first aiders in any group. One qualified person must be nominated the named first aid officer.

Keep them safe

The campaign on behalf of the Consumer Safety Unit of the Department of Trade and Industry is to stop children swallowing household chemicals. It is important that bleach is kept on the premises so that surfaces can be swabbed down after body spillage. Disinfectants, oven cleaner, lavatory cleaner and other chemicals may also be needed. Always keep all chemicals used at playgroup or nursery locked away in a cupboard.

Here is a list of things to do if you suspect that a child has swallowed a harmful substance:

1. Gently give a drink of milk. If no milk is available, give water. This dilutes the poison.
2. Do *not* make the child sick.

3. Telephone the doctor; he will tell you whether the child needs to go to hospital.
4. If you cannot contact the doctor, take the child quickly to hospital. If necessary, call an ambulance.
5. If possible, take the container and product you think has been swallowed. Do not rely on memory.
6. Try to act calmly and avoid upsetting the child.

These guidelines were laid down by the National Poisons Information Service at Guy's Hospital in London.

Other accidents

Accident Prevention and First Aid, published by the PPA, is a comprehensive guide. Buy a copy for your playgroup or nursery and use it.

Be sure you know the telephone number and address of the nearest hospital casualty department. The children's GPs should all be contactable from telephone numbers on their registration forms. If none of the helpers is a car owner or driver, often the case in a city, get the number of a reliable taxi firm. To wait for an ambulance may take too long. Keep these numbers by the telephone, so that each helper can easily find them. There may be a case for keeping a card index by the telephone too. Make a card for each child. Extract the important information from his or her registration form.

Some things to remember:

1. Every concussed child must be taken along to the nearest casualty department. This includes those who may have been unconscious for only a very short time.
2. If a bang on the head results in drowsiness, vomiting or sleep, take the child to the nearest casualty department.
3. When limbs are broken, call for an ambulance but do not move the patient.
4. When a child chokes, hold him or her upside down and hit hard between the shoulder blades. If to no avail, take the patient to casualty.
5. Always place burns or trapped fingers under running water or wrap in a wet towel.
6. Deep cuts should be seen by the GP or the casualty doctor.
7. All eye injuries should be checked by the child's GP.

Accident book and reporting accidents to your local authority

List in a case-bound book the name, date, time, nature of accident, extent of injuries, helpers present and action taken. All this information must be also put on a report of accident or serious illness of child occurring in private premises form issued by the local authority. The proprietor should sign it, date it and send it to the Social Services Department of the local authority. Always inform parents of any accidents, however small, that involve their child.

Suspected child abuse

Checklist of suspected child abuse:

1. The child has marks on his or her face or body.
2. The child's behaviour changes.
3. There is a noticeable tension between the child and his or her parent(s).
4. The child's appearance deteriorates.
5. The child fails to thrive.
6. The behaviour of the parent(s) changes.
7. The child rubs a particular part of the body often.

These changes may have other causes. All groups should behave discreetly and wisely in dealing with this subject. This is particularly important for any privately run playgroup or nursery. Ask the NSPCC for help. Do not disclose names. Get as much help and advice as possible before taking action yourself. But it is important that abused children are protected.

HIV-positive children or not?

Adopt a strict standard of hygiene in all playgroups and nurseries. It has always been important to encourage child hygiene and to limit the spread of hepatitis virus, but now it is even more important with the introduction of acquired immune deficiency syndrome (AIDS) into our society.

The National Childminding Association has published a useful pamplet on AIDS. The PPA also publishes guidelines. The virus does not live outside the body but anyone could have it. It is not spread by normal social contact - it can only be spread by sexual intercourse or infected blood.

The policy of some local authorities is that a child who is HIV positive should be able to participate in all available facilities. However, admittance of a child who is known to be HIV positive to a privately run playgroup or nursery may be another matter. This is for the proprietors of each group to decide. 'Should parents be asked?' and other awkward questions will have to be answered. Some HIV-positive children are entering the state-funded education system. Remember an HIV-positive child does not have AIDS but *does* carry the virus. Children with the actual disease will be too ill to attend and will probably be in hospital.

If a child who is HIV positive is admitted, all helpers should be informed. It may be necessary to employ an extra helper, since the child must be under constant supervision so that any accident can be dealt with quickly and efficiently.

From now on every playgroup or nursery should:

1. bag up any spilt faeces or dirty nappies;
2. disinfect any surface after a body spillage (urine, faeces, vomit or blood) with household bleach freshly diluted 1:10 in water, then dispose of immediately;
3. wash any clothes stained with blood or vomit in a 96°C wash;
4. never leave children alone with only one helper;
5. wash a cut immediately with soap and water;
6. use disposable gloves to deal with a lot of blood;
7. discourage biting;
8. cover all cuts and abrasions with waterproof dressings;
9. wash with soap and water splashes of blood on skin;
10. wash with a large quantity of water splashes of blood in eyes or mouth.

Most of these procedures are already followed by many child care facilities.

Chapter 9

Lessons or Play?

Which activities should you put out each day? Here are a few practical, simple ideas for play useful to nurseries allocating a few hours each day to play and to all playgroups. Many books have been published on play activities for the under-fives. The Pre-school Playgroups Association (PPA) has an extensive list on this subject available on request. All PPA courses cover the topic of play in detail.

The shift in emphasis as the chapter progresses is from play to lessons and more formal learning. Good nursery education is planned in advance. Children who are active and happy learners benefit from the planning of the day's activities. It is up to each child care facility to decide upon its particular emphasis. Work out a daily or weekly table of events with respect to your market: the children, their parents and the parents' expectations. Some parents want their child to be able to read by the time he or she enters primary or pre-prep school; others may be happy that their child is socialising and playing away from home.

This chapter is only a guide. It should be used in conjunction with PPA material, and information and books available at your local public library and your nearest children's library. In addition consult *Child Education* (Scholastic Publications), *Jump* (Jump), *Childsplay: A Book of Play Ideas* by Rachel Sloane (Suffolk Group Radio), *Creative Play* by Dorothy Einon (Penguin Books), *What Shall We Do Today?* by Delphine Evans (Hutchinson), *Ten Little Fingers* by Monica Stuart and Gill Soper (Faber and Faber) and *280 Ideas for Entertaining Children of All Ages* by Sheelagh Leary (Angus and Robertson).

Many materials for arts and crafts projects can be brought from home for low-budget playgroups. A range of items from fabric, old magazines, post cards, birthday and Christmas cards to pieces of wallpaper, ice cream tubs with resealable lids, yoghurt, cottage cheese or margarine tubs, egg boxes, loo roll and kitchen roll inner tubes can be used. Groups that charge high fees may have to do their collecting among the helpers and their families, since parents may be busy and not want to be bothered saving egg boxes or cereal packets. Again, work with the year's parents in mind and use your common sense.

Computer printout, used photocopying and old scrap paper provide blank surfaces on which children can draw or paint. Ask businesses in your area if they have any. Some printers sell off reel ends cheaply. DIY shops may be able to supply old pattern books and wallpaper books and others off-cuts of wood for a small charge. Many areas of the country have one or more collection points where local businesses send their discarded materials and packaging. Get the address from your public library or local enterprise agency and drive there in the hope of returning with some workable materials. Any playgroup or nursery needs an endless supply of paper.

All these resources can be used in conjunction with the equipment and consumables mentioned in Chapter 6.

Nearly everything a child does is educational in some way, so channel natural curiosity and thought.

Drawing and painting

These are probably the easiest activities to include in the day's events for all groups. All children love to partake. Learning establishments can make these activities more formal by supplying work books instead of just coloured paper and paints and crayons. Let the children make cards for occasions such as birthdays, Christmas and Easter. They will always have something to take home to mother at the end of the session, too. Children's paintings can brighten even the dullest of church halls.

Printing

Printing is an extension of painting. It can be more rewarding for some children when their pictures resemble something real. Printing blocks can be bought from some of the equipment suppliers and used with ink pads. Some inks are not always washable. Children could be supplied with painting overalls or parents asked to buy smocks.

With the help of the older children helpers could make their own printing blocks from potatoes, apples, oranges and lemons. Everyone can enjoy finger painting or bubble painting. Introduce stencils, and shapes and templates or even home-made templates from such household items as doilies.

Composite pictures

The children could all make one large picture or be divided into groups and each group make a picture. Collages that include activities such as painting, sticking, cutting, sorting and collecting can be constructed. Always supervise cutting and be aware of the numbers and positions of the scissors in circulation. Use round-tipped scissors. Home-made paste can save your group money. Other things to make are wall charts, calendars showing different festivals and holidays, and perhaps a group portrait of all the children who helped to make the picture.

Making toys, puppets and mobiles

Easter bunnies, Easter eggs to hang from the ceiling and Christmas decorations can all be made from papier maché. Make puppets from paper bags or old socks. Stage a puppet show, perhaps hosted by the older children for the younger ones. Let the older ones make the puppets and the little ones paint the scenery. A tiny town could be made from a selection of clean fruit juice cartons.

Playdough, plasticine and clay

Make your own playdough to save money. Introduce rolling pins, pastry boards and shape cutters. Children will spend hours mucking around.

Cooking

Make cold food or hot food, but never let children into the kitchen. One of the helpers will have to organise baking. On a cold day home-made hot sausage rolls could be most welcome at snack time.

Playhouse and imaginary play

All children will spend time in a well-equipped playhouse, boys *and* girls. Playing shops or pretending to be different people such as the postman or doctor is also greatly enjoyed. Dressing up is fun, too. If your budget can stretch to some dressing-up clothes there are some lovely ones on the market - dragons, monkeys and bears. Adult clothes are a good substitute, especially hats, shoes and handbags. A table with five or six out of circulation telephones is another success, but be sure to cut off any connection leads.

Sewing and threading

Early Learning Centre sells a good range of threading cards. You could also make your own using cardboard and string. Make cards of shoes with holes so that each child can practise tying knots and bows. Let the children thread objects together such as cotton reels, bottle tops, pasta quills, shells, buttons. Do not use beads or needles. Shoe laces are good for threading. Knitting is not a sensible activity for most groups since knitting needles can be dangerous and careful supervision is needed.

Many under-fives find knitting too difficult.

Singing and making music

Singing and making music should be a priority for all types of child care since all age groups benefit from them. Circle time (all children sit in a circle with a helper and sing) before snack time, lunch time or tea time is appreciated by all. It gives the other helpers time to clean up or organise meals. Sing songs that involve each child and songs where each child has to do things. It is important to teach a child to listen and do. Cassette songs are a poor substitute for the human voice, so if you can't sing hire someone who can.

Build up a good supply of musical instruments from jingle bells and drums for the very young to recorders for the older ones. *Action Songs and Finger Play* by Elizabeth Matterson (Penguin Books) has lots of ideas.

Jigsaw puzzles, picture lotto and dominoes

Making jigsaws can be a good pre-reading exercise. Simple word jigsaws matching the word with the object or the number with the number of objects can be introduced. Even the youngest children get satisfaction from having completed a jigsaw puzzle, albeit a four-piece one. Have a wide range of jigsaw puzzles. Do not underestimate children; some are very good at making jigsaw puzzles for their age.

Weighing and measuring

How many egg cups of water are needed to fill the beaker? Fun and dexterity and number skills can be developed from this exercise. Which is the heavier of two identical containers, one filled with cotton wool, the other with sand? Introduce simple balances and measuring cylinders. All children enjoy sand and water play.

Eating together

Good manners at meal times should be encouraged. Teach children how to be quiet and sit still until their snack or main meal is finished. Then train each one to ask to leave the table. Christmas parties, Easter parties, special breakfasts on a particularly cold day can all help towards this goal and be very good fun. Let the older ones help with some of the food preparation and the little ones collect the bowls or hand out the drinks.

Outdoor activities

If your playgroup or nursery has a garden, good. If not, take the children out on organised walks. Be sure to get the approval of each parent, though. Always have sufficient helpers so that supervision is good. Another alternative is to keep animals, fish or insects indoors. Do indoor gardening such as growing mustard and cress, bulbs in water and fruit stones.

Games

Skipping, hoola hoop, play tunnel burrowing, climbing, riding small trikes or pushalongs, and skittles should all be encouraged either indoors or out.

Books

Books are important for all. Make a quiet corner - the book corner. Teach each child to spend a few minutes there looking at a book each session. One of the helpers could sit in the book corner to read a story to a group of children, while another group does an activity that requires more supervision.

A good counting book should stimulate a young child's natural interest in numbers. The traditional fairy stories that lead a child into the world of make believe are as popular now as they ever were. Include a few books on having a baby, a spell in hospital, or going to the doctor, since a proportion of children from your playgroup or nursery will experience these events.

Starting school is a big moment in a child's life. Spend time on this subject. Include a few books, home-made ones if you wish, on the school day. Janet and Allan Ahlberg have written *Starting School* (Viking Kestrel).

Some children may be bilingual or speak very little English. Dual textbooks have been shown to be of little use. Encourage the bilingual child to look at books in English. Getting the child to speak may be difficult. First fix interest, perhaps by showing home-made books or playing home-made games. Those using photographs usually get some response. When the child is interested, he or she will talk. Children learn from their peers.

There are a few publications each year which review new books coming on to the market. Also a browse around your local public library might help you to choose the books to buy for your playgroup or nursery. Many libraries will loan children's books once a term. Some will send a librarian to read to the children.

Telling the time

Learning to read the face of a clock is important. You can buy story books that have a clock with hands on the front cover. You could also make your own using cardboard, clips and a piece of plastic for the hands. Then each child could have a clock on which to practise his or her skills. The concept of time is difficult for any pre-school child to grasp. Use pictures to illustrate different times of the day and show the young that the hands of a clock move clockwise.

Colours, numbers and letters

Children are often presented with these concepts in this order. Some children are number friendly, others letter friendly but it is important that the child comes in contact with these concepts daily. If he or she has a mental block with certain letters, spend more time on numbers or colours or the letters that the child knows to build up confidence. Children often know the correct answer to a question but are prevented from giving it by lack of confidence. Constant reassurance is important for any age group or child care establishment.

Memory and odd one out

Place some items on a tray or in a bucket, remove one and ask the children to tell you which one is missing. This can be made into a game of magic to hold the children's attention; or place similar objects and one different object on the tray or in the bucket. Ask the children to tell you which is the odd one out. Let each child have a turn.

Science

As an adult working with children you probably do science with them without realising it. Magnets and iron nails or pins are fun. Spend one or more sessions explaining household procedures and concepts such as electricity and water. Stress how dangerous electricity is and how a boiling kettle could cause a nasty accident. Explain and show how taps work, how locks work, how things are made. Talk about the parts of the body. Use illustrations and books to reinforce your talks. Encourage the children to ask questions.

Maps and different ethnic groups

Make maps of the world, of imaginary islands for treasure hunts, and of your own town or village. A local map with photographs or pictures of the well-known sites is another idea. Explain ethnic groups and cultures on a map of the world. To introduce fun, place a picture of each kind of regional food next to its country; for example, McDonalds next to America, a bowl of rice and chopsticks next to China, spaghetti next to Italy, and fish fingers next to Britain.

Computers

Borrow or buy a computer for your playgroup or nursery. Stick lower case letters over the keys of the keyboard. Buy educational games and programs and simple graphics packages. Some machines take a turtle which houses pens and can be programmed to draw pictures on paper on the floor. Computers are essential for children in the group who are physically handicapped.

Learning to read and write

The nursery school will place particular emphasis on these activities. Each session may include a period of time when children are seated at tables and have to do lessons. Other schools may have a slightly less formal approach, but remember that a child needs to be seated at a table to be able to control pencil and paper properly.

A child may only want to write his or her own name and nothing else before school. Teach children the conventional order and direction of each stroke. This is called print script. If you are unsure, look at work books in any bookshop. There are masses on the market. These are graded work books designed to teach language, writing and mathematical skills. Check that the progression is gradual and each book does not cover too much ground. (Oxford University Press has developed good pre-reading activity books for Early Learning Centre. Pencil, arrow and dotted line show what is to be done on each page.) It is easy and cheaper to make your own books. Never force a child into formal work too soon.

Put labels on objects around the room to help a child recognise words. Cards with pictures and words help a child to grasp the concept. Reading should never be competitive.

Playgroups may not wish to teach their children to read and write but many of their pre-reading activities will certainly help the child during his or her first term at school.

Chapter 10

Accounts

Devise a simple accounting system before your playgroup or nursery starts trading, or better still before any money is spent on the business. This is an up-to-date record of how much the business has received and how much it has spent. At any one time, using these figures and bank statements, the question 'how much money does the business actually have?' can be answered.

Receipts and payments

The amount of money a business receives is called its receipts. The amount of money it spends is called its payments. Think in terms of receipts and payments; classify each business transaction as a receipt or a payment.

Receipts

A major source of receipts is fees paid by parents. Social Services sometimes pay fees for children whose parents are not able to. An employer pays for employees' children in a few cases, which could be a subsidy to the company's workplace nursery or part payment of fees for employees' children to attend a private nursery, day nursery or creche.

Many playgroups or nurseries are owed most of their money at the beginning of term, since it is usual to bill parents termly. Fees are to be paid by the first day of term. If fees have not been recovered by the end of the third week of term, the parents should be asked to remove their child.

The refund from the Department of Social Security for money spent on milk for children is a receipt. This may be outstanding, since claims can only be made quarterly.

Fund raising is another source of receipts. Some privately funded groups, however, do not like to ask parents for financial help, although most parents and children enjoy fund-raising events.

Payments

More payments than receipts are expected. Salaries and

National Insurance contributions have to be paid, rent and heating too. Insurance, food, drink, consumables and other materials have to be purchased. During the early years, when the majority of equipment is purchased, many invoices from mail order companies and equipment suppliers may need to be paid.

Cheques will not clear immediately. But always consider you have spent the money once a cheque is written. Remember that rent may have to be paid in advance.

Here is a list of common receipts and payments. To follow convention receipts are placed on the left and payments on the right.

Receipts (income)	*Payments (expenditure)*
fees	rent
milk refund	heating
fund raising	cleaning
	salaries
	National Insurance contributions
	income tax
	milk
	food
	consumables
	other materials
	insurance
	new equipment
	repairs and replacements
	building
	loan repayments
	bank interest and charges

Under the Nurseries and Childminders Regulation Act 1948 as amended by the Health Services and Public Health Act 1968, playgroups and nurseries need not register for VAT when their turnover exceeds the VAT threshold of £23,600 per year or £8000 per quarter (1989/90). A simple system using bank statements, cheque book stubs (or paid cheques if your bank can offer this facility), bank paying-in book and proof of purchase (till receipts or invoices) for all items bought works well for a small playgroup or nursery. In addition keep a petty cash book, cash book and set of deductions working sheets. Till receipt, written receipt or invoice is used in this chapter to mean proof of purchase. Receipts are taken to mean income only.

Stationery for keeping accounts

The PPA supplies a playgroup accounts book for a few pounds. Its instructions on how to fill in the columns are good but it is confusing if the cash pages are used. Use only the bank pages towards the end of the book. This becomes your cash book.

If your business is expected to make more than 50 or 60 transactions (either receipts or payments) in its first year, more pages will be needed. Buy a cash book from any major stationers. Make sure this is a casebound analysis book A3.5 format with 14 ruled cash columns and spaces to insert headings. Books with more cash columns are available but 14 is sufficient for a small business. Some books also have printed headings but you may find it more convenient to write in your own headings by hand.

Put all petty cash transactions in a separate book. Buy a casebound lined book A5 format for petty cash. Draw vertical lines to make as many columns as you require.

Alternatively, if you spend a little more, buy a matching cash book and petty cash book. At the same time buy a pad of petty cash vouchers, a few A4 files, a pad of wages slips and two books with numbered pages in triplicate. Use one to issue written receipts to parents, etc for fees paid. Use the other as an order book in which all new materials, equipment, etc are listed when they are ordered together with the name of the supplier and price. Write each separate order on a new numbered page. This serves as a record when checking delivery notices or answering invoice queries.

Completed printed analysis tables, cash flow charts and yearly planners are all useful and can show the monthly progress of your business. Filofax publishes some good inexpensive charts, or you could make your own. Some banks supply these charts, so ask in several of your local branches.

A playgroup register filled in correctly with the name, address, telephone number and date of birth of each child in attendance is of utmost importance. The register must be taken each session. The Social Services Department of your local authority and the Department of Social Security and others will require accurate attendance numbers. The PPA playgroup register is perfectly adequate for a playgroup or even a large day nursery.

Here is a checklist of the stationery you will need to keep accounts.

- register
- cash book

- petty cash book
- petty cash box
- petty cash vouchers
- two numbered books in triplicate
- analysis tables
- cash flow/yearly planner charts
- six A4 files
- spike or stationery clip for holding petty cash vouchers
- Inland Revenue New Employers Starter Pack (see page 119)
- wages slips

Bank account

Even if most parents pay their fees with cash and you could pay most invoices or bills with cash, it is still unwise to do so. Put all cash into the business bank account and make all payments by cheque. If necessary, your business bank statements can be used by the Inland Revenue or others even before your bookkeeping procedures are properly established as a record of all business transactions that have been made.

Open a current account and deposit account for your playgroup or nursery. It is important to separate your business finances from your own personal finances as soon as possible. Most high street banks have a package for the small business. Leaflets are often available at each branch. If you live in an area where there is a choice, take out an account with the nearest branch. This will save you time and money. Remember, each transaction made at another bank costs £1.

Before your business can be considered for a bank account at a particular branch the manager will wish to see one of the following, depending on your business identity:

- if your business is a private limited company
  Memorandum and Articles of Association and certificate of incorporation of a private limited company
- if the proprietors have formed a partnership
  a legal agreement between partners
- if you are a sole trader
  a description of your playgroup or nursery
- if your business runs as a cooperative
  a set of rules and legal registration or incorporation as a cooperative

NB Voluntary groups should present a copy of their constitution and rules.

The bank manager will probably also wish to see all the following:

- a completed bank mandate (or application form) giving the names and titles of those who are allowed to sign cheques (signatories). Two signatories are required for each cheque. If there are two or more proprietors, all names can be designated signatories, any two signing each cheque. However, if you are a sole trader, you may have to think carefully about a second signatory. For a small business one signatory may be enough. Check all these details with the branch before you apply. Always keep a copy of the completed bank mandate. The officers of a private limited company are usually designated signatories. It is possible to found a private limited company with only two officers: a chairman and a secretary/treasurer;
- proof of funds;
- a brief description of the playgroup or nursery (this information can be put in a covering letter).

If you are asking for a loan, the application to the bank manager would need to be streamlined to include an annual forecast of income and expenditure over the first three years of trading and names of those who would guarantee a bank loan. Funding a business venture has been discussed in Chapter 3.

Ask if paid cheques can be returned to the business together with monthly statements. This is useful, since a photocopy of such a cheque is always proof that a particular bill was paid.

When your business is accepted as a new customer the bank will issue your paying-in books and cheque books. Make all deposits using your paying-in book. Do not waste a page, so each receipt is numbered consecutively.

A bank account is important. It enables a credit rating to be established for your business. You may be averse to borrowing money. This is wise in times of high inflation but a bank loan can help to save a struggling business.

Doing the books

An accountant might reduce your work load and give you added confidence but he or she will charge you for this work. Also he or she will insist that you keep a petty cash book, a cash book showing receipts and payments, and all till receipts, written receipts and invoices sorted according to a particular system.

Date order is an effective way of filing invoices, etc. It is also one of the easiest. Many other systems work on the date order principle too. It is best to use the same system throughout. Date order is used from here on. Unless specified otherwise, the accounts described are for a sole trader or a partnership.

You may be busy with the day-to-day running of your playgroup or nursery especially if children stay all day, so have no time in which to do the accounts; or you may be a practical person who is no good at maths. When starting a small business it is important to understand that there is a good deal of bookkeeping to be done during these first few years. If you are considering a partnership, an ideal balance is one person with a child care bias and the other a small business bias. This combination can work well - one is business manager and the other playgroup or nursery manager. This is not to say that each one cannot also do the other's job. If you are a sole trader or all partners are more interested in child care or time is precious, it is essential to employ a competent bookkeeper. Nine or ten hours of work a week should be sufficient. The bookkeeper can do the petty cash book, cash book, salaries, income tax and National Insurance contributions, and possibly the annual return and income and expenditure account, maybe eliminating the need for an accountant. Advertise in your local paper for applicants. A mother whose children are at school or playgroup might be interested. It is unwise to hire one of the mothers of the children from the group. It has been shown that mother and child do not perform to the best of their abilities if the mother works at the group. Some accounts information will almost certainly be confidential.

Petty cash

Where possible, all purchases should be made by cheque, but buying a carton of juice or a packet of biscuits for snack time from the corner shop will require cash. First decide how much money is needed for a petty cash float. This is the amount placed in the petty cash box or tin for the daily purchase of small items. Always safeguard petty cash and never have too much on the premises at once. In the examples that follow the float is £20, which is probably sufficient. Write a cheque for this amount to cash, sign it and present it to the bank teller. Ask for an assortment of change. For instance, one £5 note, nine £1 coins, five 50 pence coins, ten 20 pence coins, ten 10 pence coins, and ten 5 pence coins.

At the same time ask for a number of petty cash bags. They come in the denominations given in the right-hand column.

£20.00 of £1
£10.00 of 20 pence
£10.00 of 50 pence
£ 5.00 of 10 pence
£ 5.00 of 5 pence
£ 1.00 of 2 pence
£ 1.00 of 1 pence

Bank tellers expect change to be bagged up according to these denominations before it can be deposited in the bank. Never mix change. There may be only one 10 pence piece and one 20 pence piece among notes to be banked, but still place each coin in a separate bag.

Petty cash vouchers

Buy a book of petty cash vouchers from a stationers. Avoid the ones with a column for VAT. The only information needed is date, description, amount, authorised by, received by and a line for the total amount. Make each helper fill in onc of these vouchers each time a request for money is made. Fasten the till receipt *behind* the voucher. Authorise the amount by signature and exchange the required amount of money for the voucher. During the early years make this the responsibility of the proprietors. Keep all vouchers in date order on a spike or clip. Enter each voucher in the petty cash book. Tell all helpers that a till receipt, written receipt or invoice is needed as proof of purchase.

Petty cash voucher

Petty cash voucher			
Date	*Description*	*Amount* £	p
	Total		
Authorised by		*Received by*	

Petty cash expenditure must be properly controlled. When the float is running low, add up all the petty cash vouchers in the petty cash box. A cheque made payable to cash is then drawn for this amount. The cash is added to the existing petty cash float and the original float of £20 is restored. This system gives strict control; the vouchers and the cash added together should always equal £20. This is known as the imprest.

Entries in petty cash book

Each time an amount is drawn from the bank to restore the petty cash float to £20 it is important that the information on the vouchers reflecting the top-up amount is entered in the petty cash book.

Start on the first set of facing pages. Divide the left-hand page into five columns headed date, description, amount, from bank and in hand. Make the description column at least twice as wide as the others. The right-hand page houses the analysis columns. Divide this page into at least eight columns, one for each petty cash expense category. For instance, I use the headings milk, refreshments, equipment, cleaning materials, photocopying and stationery, telephone and postage, gas and miscellaneous. Gas needs a column because it is metered and playgroup leaders take 50 pence pieces from petty cash to feed the meter. This could be your experience too, especially if your playgroup or nursery is housed in a church hall.

On the first line in the 'Date' column put the date the first petty cash withdrawal was made from the bank. Write the cheque serial number in the 'Description' column. Insert £20.00 in the 'From bank' column.

When you make your second petty cash withdrawal equalling the total of the first batch of petty cash vouchers, make an entry on a separate line in the petty cash book for each voucher. Put the date of the first voucher in the 'Date' column. Copy the description on the voucher in the 'Description' column; for example, 'juice and milk'. Enter the total in the 'Amount' column. Then subtract this amount from £20.00 to arrive at a figure that can be placed in the 'In hand' column. The 'In hand' column will always reflect the amount of cash in the petty cash box at a particular time. Next record a breakdown of the total amount on the first petty cash voucher in the analysis columns. Here a figure will be entered in the column headed 'Milk' and one in the column headed 'Refreshments'. Follow this procedure for the next voucher and the next until all entries have been recorded.

A petty cash book showing columns and headings across two facing pages

Date	*Description*	*Amount*	*From bank*	*In hand*	*Milk*	*Refreshments*	*Equipment*	*Cleaning*	*Photocopying and stationery*	*Telephone and postage*	*Gas*	*Miscellaneous*

(*Analysis columns*: Milk to Miscellaneous)

Only the cheque for £20.00 for the petty cash float and subsequent withdrawals to restore this float to £20.00 are recorded in the cash book. The cash book records all payments made by cheque, in addition to all receipts received by the business.

Breakdown of petty cash payments

When each set of facing pages in the petty cash book is filled with entries add up all the figures in each column. The figure in the 'Amount' column must equal the totals in the analysis columns. The total in the 'From bank' column minus the total in the 'Amount' column should equal the total in the 'In hand' column. At the end of your financial year add to all the totals at the bottom of the first set of pages the respective totals on subsequent pages. These figures will become the petty cash breakdown for the year.

Here is a breakdown of petty cash spent over one tax year for a playgroup of 18 children receiving part-time care. Each item in the list heads one of the analysis columns in the petty cash book. The total for the amount spent in each category is placed next to its heading.

Petty cash breakdown

milk	11.10
refreshments	67.86
equipment	69.85
cleaning materials	8.53
photocopying/stationery	17.46
telephone/postage	1.04
miscellaneous	47.89
gas	18.50
TOTAL	242.23

Receipts *Payments* ←

Date	Description	*Total*		*Date*	*Description*	*Total*		*Milk*		*Refreshments*		*Equip-ment*		*Cleaning materials*		*Photo-copying and stationery*	
		£	p			£	p	£	p	£	p	£	p	£	p	£	p

Cash book

The cash book records all receipts and payments. Use either the PPA playgroup accounts book or an A3.5 analysis book as your cash book. If your group is in its first year, is expected to make a lot of transactions or is a large day nursery or workplace nursery, use the more expensive A3.5 version. Alternatively, you could amend the PPA playgroup accounts book to take twice as many entries. Start at the beginning of the book ignoring the cash and bank sections. Treat all pages as bank pages.

Since it cannot be used for figures, on the first right-hand page make a list of important information from the name, address, account number(s) and sorting code of your bank to names and telephone numbers of your major suppliers.

Now turn over the page. Divide this first set of double pages into columns.

The headings in your cash book should resemble those below.

Payments are divided among the analysis columns, such as those used in the petty cash breakdown, in addition to rent and heating, salaries, income tax, National Insurance contributions, insurance, building and repairs, consumables and petty cash. If you need different headings, label the correct number of columns accordingly. A completed petty cash column ensures that all cheques drawn to replenish the petty cash float appear in the cash book.

A cash book showing columns and headings running across facing pages

Analysis columns →

Telephone and postage £	p	*Gas and electricity* £	p	*Rent and heating* £	p	*Salaries, income tax and NIC* £	p	*Insurance* £	p	*Building and repairs* £	p	*Consumables* £	p	*Petty cash* £	p	*Cheque serial number*

Make entries in the cash book at the end of each day during the early days of your business. This will ensure that you forget nothing, establish a routine of sorting and storing invoices and record all receipts and payments as they are made. As you gain confidence these tasks could be saved up.

Now consider this example. Before the first day of term you have received cheques from five parents to pay their children's fees. Enter the name, amount and account number on each cheque in your paying-in book. Before you present these cheques to the bank make these entries in the receipts section of the cash book. On the first line in the first column insert the year. On the following line insert the name and the day of the month. In the 'Description' column next to the 'Date' column insert 'FEES' followed by the name on one of the cheques. In the 'Total' column that follows insert the amount on this cheque. Do the same for the next cheque, and the next and so on. On the first day of term three parents pay fees in cash. At the end of the day enter this information. Insert the name and the day of the month in the first column. In the 'Description' column that follows insert 'FEES-CASH' followed by the parent's name. Place the amount in the 'Total' column.

For example, the first eight entries in the receipts section of the cash book should look like this.

A cash book showing the receipts section only

Receipts

Date	*Description*	*Total* £	p	
1989				
April 11	FEES - K R Willison	180	00	
	FEES - T Brown	180	00	
	FEES - J Smith	180	00	
	FEES - J Gow	180	00	
	FEES - C James	180	00	
April 12	FEES - CASH - C Cowen	90	00	
	FEES - CASH - I Walton	90	00	
	FEES - CASH - C Ellerton	180	00	

Before the playgroup or nursery opens you will have spent money. Enter all these transactions which have been paid by cheque in the payments section of the cash book. Let us suppose that you have written and sent nine cheques: to the PPA for your insurance premiums, to the church for your rent for the term, to a builder to pay for alterations made to fulfil fire and safety requirements, to four major equipment suppliers for equipment and consumables, to a department store for catering equipment and to a supermarket for food, supplies and cleaning materials. On the first line in the first column of the payments section of your cash book insert the year. On the second line directly below insert the name and the day of the month. In the 'Description' column that follows insert the name to whom the cheque was made payable followed by a note of what was bought. Run over on to the next line if you wish. Be sure that sufficient detail is given so that a person unconnected with your playgroup or nursery, such as a tax inspector or auditor, can understand how the money was spent. Place the amount spent in the 'Total' column that follows. Divide this amount among the appropriate analysis columns. The payments section of the cash book is illustrated on pages 112-13.

Each day fill in receipts and payments. When you reach the end of a page add up all the figures in each column. When all the totals in the analysis columns are added together this figure should equal the total in the 'Total' column on the payments side. Using all these separate totals at the end of the tax year an income and expenditure account can be drawn up.

Preparing annual accounts

Annual accounts, which include an income and expenditure account and petty cash breakdown, are important. They can tell you how efficient your playgroup or nursery is in meeting its aims; inform parents who have been asked to help how successful your group has been at fund raising; show how much revenue must be raised during the next financial year; immediately show by how much annual income is more or less than expenditure; can be used as part of a package to a bank or an enterprise agency in the hope of raising extra funds and show how much income tax is paid each year.

If your playgroup or nursery is trading as a private limited company, a copy of your annual accounts must be lodged with the Registrar of Companies. They must include a balance sheet and a directors' report. The accounts must first be audited by a

A cash book showing the payments section

Payments ←

Date	*Description*	*Total* £	p	*Milk* £	p	*Refreshments* £	p	*Equipment* £	p	*Cleaning materials* £	p	*Photocopying and stationery* £	p
1989													
April 11	PPA - insurance 3/89 to 3/90	43	25										
	St Mary's - rent 21/3/89 to 21/6/89	300	00										
	J J Jones - building	500	00										
	Galt - sand tray	80	33					80	33				
	Community Playthings - stove, sink	126	40					126	40				
	Early Learning Centre - play tunnel	16	99					16	99				
	Nottingham Educational Supplies - paint, paper, craft books, scissors	69	76					14	89				
	J Lewis - children's bowls, mugs, kettle	61	79					61	79				
	J Sainsbury - coffee, biscuits, cleaning materials	40	74			24	75			15	99		
		1,239	26	-	-	24	75	300	40	15	99	-	-

chartered accountant. This can cost several hundred pounds. If this annual return is not filed, the company could be struck off the register and to reinstate a company is a lengthy and costly procedure.

A balance sheet summarises the business's assets, liabilities and capital at the end of its year of trading. It automatically highlights any financial problems. An example is given in the last right-hand page of the PPA playgroup accounts book. If you wish to know more about how to prepare a balance sheet, consult *Financial Management for the Small Business* by Colin Barrow (Kogan Page).

Regardless of business identity, keep the books for at least seven years just in case your playgroup or nursery receives a visit from the Collector of Taxes.

Income and expenditure account for the first year of trading

To make an income and expenditure account for your playgroup or nursery take a sheet of journal paper and on the top left-hand side write 'receipts'; on the top right-hand side write 'payments'.

Analysis columns →

Telephone and postage		Gas and elecricity		Rent and heating		Salaries, income tax, and NIC		Insurance		Building and repairs		Consumables (paint, paper)		Petty cash		Cheque serial number
£	p	£	p	£	p	£	p	£	p	£	p	£	p	£	p	
								43	25							000001
				300	00											000002
										500	00					000003
																000004
																000005
																000006
												54	87			000007
																000008
																000009
-	-	-	-	300	00	-	-	43	25	500	00	54	87	-	-	

Below receipts write the receipt headings from the cash book, each on a separate line. From the total column on the receipts side of the cash book take a separate total for each of these categories and insert the figure.

Next list under payments all the categories used as headings to the analysis columns in the cash book. Add up all the figures in each of these analysis columns. Place each separate amount on the correct line. It may be helpful to work through this procedure while referring to the completed income and expenditure account on page 114.

Filling in the payments side should be easy. If you are in the habit of adding up the figures in each column once each set of facing pages is filled with figures in the cash book, at the end of the tax year just add together each set of totals. For example, if you have used five sets of facing pages, there will be five subtotals for each category.

Now add up the column of figures on the receipts side and the column of figures on the payments side. Place the totals on the same line but on their correct sides. In the example on page 114

Income and expenditure account for the first year of trading

1987 1988 £	*Receipts*	1988 1989 £	1987 1988 £	*Payments*	1988 1989 £
-	Fees	7,200.00	-	Milk	300.00
	Fund raising	516.30		Refreshments	103.80
				Equipment	2,628.99
	Milk refund	311.10		Cleaning materials	96.25
				Photocopying and stationery	128.99
				Telephone and postage	169.75
				Gas and electricity	105.83
				Rent and heating	990.00
				Salaries and NIC	2,639.96
				Insurance/PPA	43.25
				Building and repairs	50.00
				Consumables	131.98
				Petty cash	242.23
	Total	8,027.40		Total	7,631.03
				Surplus for year carried down	396.37
		8,027.40			8,027.40
	Surplus for year brought down	396.37		Accumulated surplus carried forward to next year	396.37
		396.37			396.37

the total is £8027.40 on the receipts side (annual turnover) and £7631.03 on the payments side. Subtract the smaller sum from the larger to determine in this case the profit for the year, £396.37. This amount is written as a surplus on the payments side.

In any income and expenditure account both sides must balance. Here the surplus and the total on the payments side must equal the total on the receipts side. The difference between the totals of the two sides makes both sides add up to the same figure. This is true for a loss (deficit) as well as for a profit (surplus) but remember in any one tax year this account can only show one, loss or profit.

Next insert the surplus below the total on the payments side. On a new line below bring down the receipts total on the left-hand side and payments total to include the surplus on the right-hand side. Below this line insert the surplus on both sides twice more.

If you cannot make both sides of the income and expenditure account balance, recheck your addition. If a discrepancy remains, check each entry in the cash book and petty cash book carefully.

This turnover of £8027.40 a year is small but realistic for a playgroup housed in a church hall taking 18 children for five morning sessions a week during term time only. The two proprietors receive a small salary (£400 a year each) but the paid helper who is necessary to maintain the correct child to helper ratio is paid PPA rates. Each child is charged £2 a session. The surplus of £396.37 at the end of the year can be treated as extra income for the proprietors and divided equally between them. If a profit-sharing scheme is under way, this amount would be divided among the proprietors and the paid helper.

Your bank statement

Your first bank statement might look something like the one on page 116. This statement is set out in the same way as the cash book with an additional column headed 'Balance'. However, the payments column (debits) and the receipts column (credits) are transposed. The balance column shows how much is left in the bank account at the end of the day's transactions. An overdraft is denoted D or DR. Money in the account is denoted C or CR, that is the account is in credit.

Abbreviations are explained on the statement. Interest to date is usually spelled out followed by the amount in the payments column. Bank charges are often described as service charges. Again the amount is placed in the payments column. Some banks indicate a deposit as sundries in the description column. Other banks place TR followed by the number on the paying-in slip in

Your monthly bank statement

Date	*Description*	*Payments*	*Receipts*	*Balance*
NOV 10	BALANCE BROUGHT FORWARD			909.56C
NOV 16	000002	153.33		
NOV 16	000003	9.20		
NOV 16	000004	50.00		
NOV 16	SUNDRIES		28.25	725.28C
NOV 17	000001	120.00		605.28C
NOV 21	000005	92.67		
NOV 21	000006	9.20		503.41C
NOV 28	000008	15.00		488.41C
DEC 5	000009	40.00		
DEC 5	SC	8.00		440.41C
DEC 9	BALANCE CARRIED FORWARD			440.41C

the description column. The amount is always placed in the receipts column.

The numbers in this balance column may differ from those in the cash book at any one time. For example, a cheque to a major equipment supplier is entered in the payments column of the cash book on the day it is sent to the company. The bank account will not show this transaction until the cheque has been received by the supplier, banked and cleared by your bank, a period of up to one week perhaps. This cheque shows up as outstanding in the cash book (that is, the entry has not been ticked off) until it has been presented to the bank. As long as there are outstanding cheques the bank statement will differ from the cash book.

Prepare a bank reconciliation statement each month. This is a record that the balances in the bank statement and those in the cash book are the same when the outstanding and unrecorded items are taken into account. Compile a table similar to the one that follows. The numbers are taken from the given bank statement. Two entries, a cheque for £50 to Galt (cheque serial number 000007) and bankings of £180.00 in cash, were made too late to show up in the bank statement. Bank charges, standing orders and direct debits are not recorded in the cash book.

Bank reconciliation statement

	Debit	Credit
Proprietor's version of the bank balance	578.41	
All unrecorded items (not yet shown in the cash book)		
bank charges (SC)		8.00
All outstanding items (not yet shown on the bank statement)		
cheque no 000007 to Galt	50.00	
bankings in cash		180.00
Bank's version of the bank balance		440.41
TOTAL	628.41	628.41

When the amounts on the total line balance the bank statement is reconciled.

Sending out the term's accounts

It is usual to bill parents for children's fees at the end of term for the next term, payable by the beginning of the new term. Send out a simple account for each child. A specimen is given on page 118. Using a sheet of your headed paper, type the child's name in full at the top of the page followed by fee account for spring, summer or winter term. If each child has been allocated an account number, place this after the child's name. For instance, 00089/02 - the child's account number is 00089 and /02 means that this bill is for the child's second term.

Now give a breakdown of costs followed by the total amount payable. Below the total clearly state the conditions of payment, for instance when the account has to be paid, to whom the cheque must be made payable and to whom it should be sent. Remember if a cheque is made out incorrectly, it will not be cleared by your bank and a charge will be rendered. Some banks charge £2.50 for a returned cheque.

Give details of how to obtain a written receipt. When a written receipt is requested by a parent make out an entry giving the name and account number of the child, the total amount of money paid and the date on which the account was settled in the numbered book in triplicate used for this purpose. Keep two copies. Send the top copy to the person who made the request or hand it to one of the family on the first day of term.

Finally, state at the bottom of the page in large type how much notice must be given. It is usual to expect one term's notice for each child.

Below is a sample account for a child who is charged on a sessional basis. If the fees are fixed for the entire term, delete the line that says *x* weeks at £00.00 per week. Instead replace it with TOTAL and give the total amount for the term.

____________________ Playgroup/Nursery School

____

Telephone ______________________________

(Names and addresses of proprietors)

John Smith (Account number 00089/02)
Fee account for winter term

Day of the week		*Amount* £ p
Monday	half day/all day	
Tuesday	half day/all day	
Wednesday	half day/all day	
Thursday	half day/all day	
Friday	half day/all day	
x weeks at £00 per week		
plus extras		
minus deposit		
TOTAL		

Please make each cheque payable to __________________ Playgroup/ Nursery School and send it to the proprietor ______________________
at ____
on or before the first day of term.
Write your child's name and account number on the reverse of the cheque.
Ask if you require a written receipt. It will be handed to one of your family on the first day of term unless you enclose a stamped addressed envelope.

ONE ENTIRE TERM'S NOTICE IS REQUIRED FOR EACH CHILD.

Paying invoices

Check each invoice carefully. During the early years of the business you will almost certainly receive many invoices from equipment suppliers. When the goods are despatched you should receive a delivery notice. Check the information on the delivery notice against the order book in which you should have recorded all the relevant information before an order is placed. If there is a discrepancy, contact the supplier.

Once checked place the delivery notice preceding its page in the order book. When the invoice arrives (usually a few days later) check the invoice against the order book and the delivery notice. If the information is correct, make a cheque payable to the company in question for the correct amount. Write your account number and invoice number on the back of the cheque and send it together with any paying-in slip (often at the bottom or the side of the invoice) to the correct address.

Mark on your section of the invoice that this bill has been paid, giving the date and serial number on the cheque. Make an entry for this amount in the payments section of the cash book. The delivery note can then be taken from the order book and stapled to the back of your portion of the invoice. Sort and store the invoice. Write at the bottom of the correct page in the order book that the invoice has been paid, giving the date and the cheque serial number. Strike a diagonal line across the page, so that at a glance you can see if an order has been paid or not.

For a small business there is no need to keep a cheques issued book as your cheque book stubs record this information.

Salaries: Inland Revenue New Employers Starter Pack

The Inland Revenue New Employers Starter Pack is invaluable. Apply for one from your local tax office even if helpers are paid less than National Insurance contribution or PAYE tax thresholds. The contents of the pack are listed below, and some of the more important procedures described in detail.

- *PAYE Tax Tables A–F*

These *PAYE Tax Tables* will continue in use until the tax office tells you to destroy them. They are essential if helpers pay income tax, since you will need to refer to one or more each time you write salary cheques or make up pay packets.

- *Notes on Expenses, Payments and Benefits for Directors and Certain Employees 480*

- *Thinking of Taking Someone On IR53*

This is a good introduction to the subject.

- *Employer's Guide to National Insurance Contributions NP.15*

This guide is comprehensive. Part A gives fundamental information on such things as how to get a new employee's National Insurance number, how to record all National Insurance contributions, how to complete an end of year return, and how to complete an employee's annual statement, declaration and certificate. Procedures used less often are described in Part B.

- *National Insurance (NI) Contribution Tables CF391 and CF392*

If helpers are paid more than £43 per week (1989/90) you will need to refer to these tables when you write salary cheques or make up pay packets.

- *Employer's Guide to Statutory Maternity Pay NI.257*

This is a summary of the scheme. It gives a chart of all the necessary procedures. Statutory maternity pay is a scheme for most women employees to get a basic amount of maternity pay from their employers. To be part of this scheme the helper's earnings must be sufficiently high for the employer to pay Class 1 NIC. This condition excludes many playgroup leaders and helpers.

The other reasons why the employer cannot pay statutory maternity pay are that the helper

1. was not employed by the playgroup or nursery for long enough;
2. did not say soon enough that she would be away from work;
3. did not give medical evidence soon enough;
4. did not tell the playgroup or nursery soon enough that she had had her baby;
5. was out of the European Community;
6. was in legal custody.

Statutory maternity pay is payable for 18 weeks. There is a higher rate and a lower rate. A helper who has worked for you for at least six months before the qualifying week (the 15th week before her maternity certificate Mat B1 states the baby is due) gets the lower rate. However, if she has worked for you continuously for more than two years or five years part time, she is entitled to the higher rate for six weeks of the maternity pay period.

If your helper is not eligible for this benefit, a maternity allowance from the Department of Social Security may be available. Complete form SMP.1 and give it to her. She must complete a form MA1 and send these forms with her maternity certificate Mat B1 to her local office.

Sections 20, 24–27, 43–57, 69 and Appendix 1 tell you when and how to pay statutory maternity pay and how to claim back the SMP you have paid. It is unlikely that you will need to follow these procedures during the first year of your business.

- *Statutory Sick Pay (SSP)/Statutory Maternity Pay (SMP) SSP/SMP55*

This booklet gives rates, notes and tables of dates. A useful chart called a quick guide to statutory sick pay is included. Statutory sick pay need not be paid to a helper who has been away sick for less than four consecutive days. Weekly earnings must be £84.00 (1989/90) or more to qualify for the weekly statutory sick pay rate of £52.10 (standard) and between £43.00 and £84.00 (1989/90) to qualify for the lower rate of £36.25. Again, playgroup leaders or helpers who are paid less than £43.00 a week cannot benefit from this scheme. Some of the other exclusion reasons are that she is 60 years of age or her contract of service is for a period of three months or less. For the reasons written in small print, refer to the *Employer's Guide to Statutory Sick Pay NI.227* and to Sections 120–134 and Appendix 1 on how much to pay, when and how to make payment, and how to claim back the statutory sick pay you have paid.

As an employer you will be required to complete a form SSPI(E) if your helper is not eligible for this benefit. Fortunately, she may be able to claim sickness benefit or invalidity benefit from the Department of Social Security. In this event she should complete pages 3, 4, 5 and 6 of this form. When you order form SSPI(E) also order form SSPI(T).

- *Employer's Guide to Statutory Sick Pay NI.227*

- *National Insurance Contribution Rates, Statutory Sick Pay and Statutory Maternity Pay Rates NI.208*

This is a concise guide which gives all relevant weekly earnings necessary to qualify for benefits.

- *Employer's Guide to PAYE P7*

This guide tells you all you need to know about pay as you earn. There are useful sections on what to do at different times of the year, the different types of payments and deductions, and what to do in particular circumstances. It has a good index which makes finding specific information easy.

- *Notes P8*

These are extremely useful sheets which tell you how to operate a pay as you earn (PAYE) scheme.

- *Deductions Working Sheet P11*

A completed deductions working sheet for each helper is the only record of salaries and deductions needed by a small playgroup or nursery. Always have a few spare sheets available. Helpers can leave suddenly and new sheets will be required then and on 6 April each year.

- Form P45 Details of Employee Leaving

Form P45 procedures are discussed in detail below.

- Form P46

Form P46 procedures are discussed together with form P45 procedures.

- *Deduction of Tax and National Insurance Contributions from Pay P24(T)*

- Employer's Permanent Record of Employees P13

- Employee's Coding Claim P15

- Details of Directors P222

- Reply Envelopes Addressed to HM Inspector of Taxes ENVBR8

- Employer's Stationery Order Form P34

When completing an order, be sure to order enough forms for the following six months. The names of the forms you require that are not given on this form can be written on the blank lines at the end of the form. Any forms mentioned in this section can be requested. Copies of guides are available free from: DSS Leaflets, PO Box 21, Stanmore, Middlesex HA7 1AY.

Registration with the Collector of Taxes

Once you have notified your tax office or requested an Inland Revenue New Employers Starter Pack you will be informed of your tax district, and will be given a reference number. Upon registration with the Collector of Taxes a payslip booklet P30BC(Z) carrying another reference number will be despatched. Use this booklet to pay any National Insurance contributions or income tax by cheque, Bank Giro, National Girobank Transfer or at the post office. Each payslip shows the period covered and the date on which payment is due.

Each year you will automatically receive a Budget update giving new thresholds laid down in the Budget. For example:

1. the emergency code is 278L W1/M1 (1989/90);
2. the PAYE monthly threshold is £232.00 (1989/90);
3. the National Insurance lower earnings limit is £43.00 per week (1989/90).

Any new *PAYE Tax Tables* are usually enclosed. Sheet 2 of *Notes P8*, a new deductions guide, is often replaced.

Form P45 or P46

When a helper starts working for you ask for her National Insurance number and parts 2 and 3 of her form P45. If she has forgotten or lost her National Insurance number or does not have one because she has never worked before, follow the procedure given in Part A of the *Employer's Guide to National Insurance Contributions NP.15.*

Take parts 2 and 3 of her form P45 and check that items 5 and 6 agree on both copies. If they do not, notify your local tax office immediately. The tax code is given as item 5, the last entries on the deductions working sheet as item 6. A helper's tax code or PAYE code reflects the tax allowance to which she is entitled. It is made up of one or more numbers and a letter. Refer to *PAYE Tax Tables* for examples and Sheet 2 of *Notes P8.*

Check that item 2, her National Insurance number, has been inserted correctly. Never alter any information on any form P45 you are given unless asked to do so by HM Inspector of Taxes.

Once you have transferred the information from her form P45 to a deductions working sheet, detach part 3 having completed items 7 to 14, and send it to your local tax office. Keep part 2 tucked inside the deductions working sheet.

She may not have a form P45. This is likely if she has not worked recently or has been earning only a small wage. Ask her to complete certificate A (if this is her first regular job since leaving full-time education and she has not claimed unemployment benefit) or B (if this is her main job and she has other income) on form P46. Complete the reverse of the form yourself. You could ask each new helper to complete two forms just in case one is lost. Always write in capitals on any printed form.

If your helper is paid below the PAYE threshold, withhold the signed form P46 and deduct no income tax each pay day. But if she earns more than £232.00 (1989/90) a month, she will be liable for income tax on anything above this amount. So send her signed form P46 with certificate A or B completed to HM Inspector of Taxes at your local tax office. Give her a coding claim form P15 to complete, having first inserted her National Insurance number and the tax office reference number for your playgroup or nursery. The form is clearly laid out and easy to complete. Until you have heard from the tax office you must use the emergency code (278L) (1989/90) and deduct the correct amount of income tax each pay day.

When a helper is promoted and her salary is increased above the PAYE threshold, complete a form P46. She need not complete certificate A or B. Send the form P46 to HM Inspector of Taxes, but do not deduct income tax until you are told to do so by your tax office. Do not give her a coding claim form P15.

When a helper leaves, you must complete a clean form P45 for her to present to her new employer. Refer to Sheet 5 of *Notes P8* which describes this procedure clearly. Retain page 1 and send it immediately to your local tax office. Give parts 2 and 3 to your helper with her last pay packet. Your playgroup or nursery may not lose a helper during its first year but it is wise to familiarise yourself with this procedure.

PAYE and National Insurance contributions

You will spend less time doing the salaries if your helpers work part time or are paid less than the PAYE and National Insurance contribution thresholds. All you have to do is to write a cheque for the correct amount of money or pay the helper in cash, complete a wages slip and follow Sections D43 to D45 of the *Employer's Guide to PAYE P7*.

This is an unlikely situation for a day nursery or creche which is open all day. It may be possible to have two shifts of part-time helpers but it means that the children will have more faces to learn and there might be a greater turnover of helpers because of their increased numbers. A playgroup or nursery school opening only one session a day or taking each child for only one session a day could manage with a part-time workforce.

It is a legal requirement that each employee receives a written statement of gross pay, deductions and net pay each pay day. Many helpers will not be required to work during the holidays. Often they are paid half salary for these weeks. Since no one wants to receive a monthly or weekly salary that varies in amount, it is better to divide the salary due over the year into 12 or 52 equal portions. An exception is the helper in the day nursery, creche or workplace nursery who works during the school holidays.

The low-paid helper's net monthly (or weekly) pay will equal her gross monthly (or weekly) pay since no deductions are made. The higher earner who receives between £43.00 and £53.00 a week is liable for National Insurance contributions but no income tax.

Those who earn more than £232.00 a month (1989/90) must pay National Insurance contributions and income tax. The basic rate of income tax is 25 per cent.

The first £2785 (1989/90) is tax free. This amount is called the single person's allowance. The married man's allowance is £4375 (1989/90). Once a helper earns more than £20,700 the higher rate of 40 per cent tax is payable. This is unlikely, but perhaps in the case of a manager of a workplace nursery or creche it is not.

Hourly payment and overtime

It is best to discourage time sheet payment; that is, paying helpers by the hour. Paying overtime can be another burden. If a helper is required to cover for another, it may easier for her to be given time off *in lieu*. But remember the correct child to helper ratio must be maintained at all times.

Deducting National Insurance contributions

When working out amounts to deduct for income tax or National Insurance contributions think in terms of W1 or M1 (see page 128). The *Free Pay Tables, Table A*, lists amounts for these periods. For example, M1 means month 1 and spans 6 April to 5 May. For the remainder of this chapter helpers are paid monthly.

For helpers who are between the ages of 16 and 60 refer to *National Insurance (NI) Contribution Tables Not Contracted-Out Contributions CF391.* To determine how much to deduct, look down the far left-hand column until you find the amount of money your helper is paid each month. If you cannot find the exact amount, work to the nearest figure under. Run your finger along the line until you find the total contribution payable, the employee's contribution and the employer's contribution.

Some married women and widows may be eligible for reduced rate contributions.

Those playgroups and nurseries that have a contracted-out scheme in operation should determine contributions using *National Insurance (NI) Contribution Tables CF392.*

If you are in any doubt as to the correct operation of PAYE you should consult your local tax office as Section A2 of the *Employer's Guide to PAYE P7* recommends.

Deducting PAYE (income tax)

Locate your *PAYE Tax Tables A–F. Table A* is used to work out free pay to date for those helpers whose tax code has a suffix H, L, P, T or V (not code NT). When making up salaries for helpers with other codes first refer to *Tables B–D.*

Open *Table A* and look down the far left-hand column under code until you hit the helper's tax code. Ignore its suffix. Run your finger along the line to the next figure which is free pay to date. To find taxable pay to date subtract free pay to date from gross pay to date. If the total is a minus figure, this means an income tax refund is due. Check with your local tax office before you issue a refund and never issue one if your helper has only worked in your playgroup or nursery for one month.

Now determine how much income tax is due from taxable pay to date. Refer to page 2 of Sheet 2 of *Notes P8* to know when to use *Tables C–D* instead of *Table B* to determine income tax payable. Always scale down the amount, that is ignore the pence.

This example is based on tax tables and emergency code (260L) for 1988/89.

	M1	*M2*
Total basic pay	£380.00	£380.00
Total pay to date	£380.00	£760.00
Total free pay to date from *Table A*	£217.42	£434.84

Total taxable pay to date	£162.58	£325.16
Total tax due from *Table B*	£ 40.50	£ 87.75*
Tax	£ 40.50	£ 47.25

* This figure can cause confusion. During the second and subsequent months of employment the figure for total tax due includes income tax to be paid for the month in question plus the income tax already paid during the year. Therefore, to determine the amount of income tax to be paid during the month in question, subtract total tax due for the previous month from total tax due for this month. In this example subtract £40.50 from £87.75 which equals £47.25.

Pay all income tax to the Collector of Taxes promptly as described on page 123.

Wages slips

Here is a wages slip.

Week or month number M1	*Date* 30 April
Name: Susan Brown	
Gross pay	£177.62
Superannuation	
Gross pay for tax purposes	£177.62
Gross pay to date for tax purposes	£177.62
Tax-free pay	£217.42
Taxable pay to date	
Tax due to date	
Tax refund	
Tax	
Employee's NIC	
Other deductions	
Total deductions	
Net pay	£177.62
Holiday pay	
Total amount payable	£177.62
Employer's NIC	
Employer's and employee's NIC	
Contracted-out contribution	
Holiday scheme	

Write two wages slips for each helper each pay day. Keep one copy inside her deductions working sheet once you have made the month's entries. A pad of wages slips can be bought from any large stationers.

Deductions working sheet P11

A deductions working sheet updated each pay day for each helper is an adequate salary record. The Inland Revenue require it for all except the low paid.

If possible pay your helpers on a monthly basis. The deductions working sheet looks the same from the front and the back, with one difference; one side houses lines for the dates from 6 April to 5 November (M1 to M7) and the other side from 6 November to 5 April (M8 to M12). Each month is given a number from 1 to 12. Month 1 (M1) is from 6 April until 5 May. The information on the top of the form is general and the 14 columns below are blank for details of salary and deductions to be inserted.

To complete the top section extract the information from the helper's form P45. First insert the name of your playgroup or nursery, then its tax district and reference, the year ending on 5 April, the helper's surname and forenames, her National Insurance number and date of birth. Let the section date of leaving remain blank. Insert her tax code and amended code if you have been told to do so by the Inland Revenue. There is also a box to insert the number for occupational pension schemes newly contracted-out since 1 January 1986 and one to insert the *National Insurance Contribution Table* letter.

Each pay day insert figures for National Insurance contributions on the left-hand side and those for income tax on the right-hand side of each employee's sheet.

End of year return

After 5 April complete an end of year return P14 for each helper still employed by your playgroup or nursery. Send the first two pages in separate bundles to HM Inspector of Taxes. Give the last page, P60, to your helper. There is a loose sheet included in the Inland Revenue New Employers Starter Pack which clearly illustrates how to complete an end of year return.

The employer's supplementary return, annual statement, declaration and certificate will be sent to you, together with a sheet to list those helpers who are paid less than £43 a week (1989/90) or work for your playgroup or nursery on a casual basis. Complete these forms after 5 April. Comprehensive instructions are usually included but the forms are easy to follow.

All the figures needed to complete these forms are given in the deductions working sheets, if they have been completed correctly and pay and tax totals inserted on 5 April. Totals for statutory sick pay and statutory maternity pay should also be included if the playgroup or nursery is covered by these schemes.

Computerisation

Have you thought of running your payroll on computer? For a large nursery or creche this could save time. More details are given in *Computerised Payroll IR70* which can be obtained free of charge from any tax office.

The Collector of Taxes PAYE audit

Names are thrown up by the Inland Revenue's computer. If the name of your playgroup or nursery is chosen, the Inland Revenue will give you sufficient time to get your books in order. First you will receive a form allowing you to choose a time that suits you. Be sure to give yourself enough time.

On the day of the audit lay out on a large table or desk the cash book; petty cash book; fees book and register; file containing till receipts, written receipts and invoices; petty cash vouchers (with till receipts attached); paying-in book(s) and cheque book(s) and sheets showing income and expenditure account, petty cash breakdown and inventory of major equipment. Place the deductions working sheets for all helpers in a neat pile at the front. Check that an up-to-date deductions working sheet, with form P45 or form P46 and duplicate wages slips tucked inside, is available for each helper. Place your PAYE/National Insurance contributions paying-in book on top.

Make the officer feel welcome when he (or she) arrives. Offer a cup of coffee, while briefly describing the workings of your playgroup or nursery. Then leave the room allowing the officer to look through the books at ease. Once he is satisfied that the accounts are correct, he will ascertain how much you have paid in salaries during the financial year in question and that the correct amount of income tax and National Insurance contributions have been paid to the Inland Revenue. If a discrepancy is found, he will go through the books concerned with you.

Income tax must be deducted if the employee has other employment, however infrequent. Therefore, you must have a signed form P46 or a form P45 (see page 124) for each employee or recovery of income tax at basic rate will be made by the officer even if her monthly or weekly salary is below the monthly or weekly PAYE and National Insurance contribution thresholds.

So as proprietors you will have to pay income tax out of your profits. It is unlikely that you will be able to recover this amount.

If everything balances, the officer will look at the income and expenditure account for your playgroup or nursery for an accumulated surplus carried forward to next year. This will be treated as income to the proprietors and they will then have to pay income tax on it. The rate is determined by how much they have already paid themselves throughout the financial year in question if a partnership, sole trader or cooperative. If your playgroup or nursery is trading as a private limited company, corporation tax is payable on this amount at a rate of 25 per cent if annual turnover is £150,000 or less.

Chapter 11

Childminding

A registered childminder is a person paid to look after somebody else's children in her own home for more than two hours a day. She need not register with the Social Services Department of the local authority for the area in which she lives if she looks after a relative's child or any child for *less* than two hours a day.

If you find your own children demanding, both physically and mentally, childminding is probably not the job for you. However, if you love small children, their noise, mess, affection and constant questions, this career can generate a moderate income and allow you time to look after your own children as well. Start-up expense is low, especially if you have small children of your own, as you will not need to buy toys, books, and games and other equipment such as a highchair, cot, and pram or buggy. Those without small children can keep costs down by buying second-hand equipment from advertisements placed in the local press and newsagents' windows. Often the most expensive and useful piece of equipment is a double buggy. If you drive a car, fit baby seats or safety harnesses to the back seat. Baby seats cost between £20 and £50. Some hospitals, clinics and shops hire them out for periods of six to nine months. The charge is likely to be over £10, so if you are planning a full-time childminding career it is almost certainly better value to buy seats and harnesses. Consult your health visitor or local road safety officer if you do wish to rent. Telephone 0800 234888 for the Department of Transport's free leaflet entitled *Protect Your Child in the Car*. Also, the Child Accident Prevention Trust publishes a useful leaflet *First Ride Safe Ride: Keeping Your Baby Safe in the Car*.

It is a real advantage if you live in a house or a flat with a garden that can take a swing, sandpit and, if possible, a climbing frame. This might mean that you will find it easier to get children if other local childminders do not have gardens. Very often families in cities live in flats without gardens. In this case, you must stress to parents that you can take the children to a local park, playground or outdoor under-fives group once or twice a week. However, some parents feel insecure if they do not know the whereabouts of their child at all times, so they will not give permission for their child to be taken out. Always check with the parents, and be sure to get a parent's signature on the agreement between parent and childminder if they give their permission.

Childminding might suit the non-working lone parent. The Department of Social Security recognises that this is a job involving daily expenses. Therefore, for those claiming Income Support or Family Credit, benefit might only be reduced by a few pounds. Read the section below on profits. If you are still unsure, do not register until you have talked to the pre-school adviser for your area at your Social Services Department. An advice worker at the national centre of Gingerbread, the association for lone parents and children, might also be able to answer your questions.

Registration

If you wish to register as a childminder, you must complete a form for the private day care sector to comply with the Nurseries and Childminders Regulations Act 1948 as amended by the Health Services and Public Health Act 1968. You can obtain a form from the Social Services Department of your local authority; the telephone number will be in your local telephone directory. When you make your call introduce yourself as a new childminder wishing to register, and ask to speak to the appropriate person, usually the pre-school adviser. The regulations and organisation of each local authority vary across the country. Be sure to give the town where you live since there may be more than one pre-school adviser in the same office, each adviser being responsible for one part of the region.

You will have to give information about any court conviction, including probation or a conditional discharge, or summons brought against you that has not been disposed of, criminal offences, your health and the health of your family. You must also give your consent for the Social Work Department, health visitor, police and Housing Department to be contacted, and reports obtained from them. Finally, a declaration on conduct and corporal punishment, consent to talk to your doctor if necessary, and an affirmation that no children have been removed from your care must be signed by you.

All those working with children must be thoroughly vetted by the police. This may take some time but it is really only a matter of the police running the name and details of the childminder through their computer. The other members of any childminder's household are also vetted. This is nothing to be worried about; remember that you are not being singled out.

Expect a social worker to visit your home to talk to you and check on facilities such as loos and kitchen.

Social Services are often very helpful, so do not be put off by someone 'inspecting' your home. Everything will probably be fine. Once your registration has been approved, you will be issued with a certificate and a registration number. *Then* you can start minding children, but not before. Your name and address will be placed on your region's list of registered childminders.

Insurance

It is important that you are covered by an insurance policy. If you look after somebody else's children you must be covered in case of an accident. Premiums are usually only a few pounds each year. Social Services will be able to recommend a good policy. The National Childminding Association can supply comprehensive cover to its members together with other useful advice. You can obtain a membership form by telephoning or writing to the Association. The annual membership fee is £8.50 (1989/90) and £12.75 to include the insurance premium. These rates are increased slightly each year. The Pre-school Playgroups Association (PPA) offers insurance under its group policy for up to five children. Unfortunately, cover is reduced to public liability only.

Lunches and other meals

Many childminders include a cold lunch in the hourly rate if the child is there at lunch time. Drinks are not usually rationed but often biscuits are. Children are expected to leave home having had a good breakfast. A mid-morning snack of a piece of fruit or biscuit is usually provided and again a light tea. For those children who have not been collected by 4.00 pm and stay to supper or high tea a cooked meal ought to be provided but you could charge a small amount for this. In fact, if you like cooking, it might be better to included a cooked lunch and high tea for the children and charge a marginally higher hourly rate. Be warned that some parents might object to paying for extras, so it is better to sort out these details at the agreement between parent and childminder stage when the hourly rate is fixed.

Agreement between parent and childminder

Be sure to state all the terms clearly on the agreement before the

AGREEMENT BETWEEN PARENT AND CHILDMINDER

Name of childminder ________________________________

Address ________________________________

Telephone number ________________________________

Registered by ____________________ Social Services Department

Registration No ________________________________

Child's name ________________________________

Hours

MONDAY TUESDAY WEDNESDAY THURSDAY FRIDAY

Meals ________________________________

Fees £_____ per week/£_____ per day/£_____ per hour
After _____ pm and weekends £_____ per hour
For periods of less than 4 hours £_____ per hour
Charges for absence because of
Sickness £_____
Occasional days off £_____
Parents' holidays £_____
Childminder's holidays £_____
Other _________ £_____

Pay _________ in advance/daily/weekly
Playgroup/under-fives fees to be paid by ____________________

Parents to provide ________________________________

Any special arrangements ________________________________

When the child is ill, he/she can attend only at the childminder's discretion.

This agreement will be reviewed on ____________________

____________________ ____________________

Parent's signature (followed by name, address and tel no) — Childminder's signature

____

Date

child starts coming to you. The National Childminding Association will supply you with ten agreement forms for a small sum which works out cheaper than typing up your own form and photocopying it, as most photocopies cost 10 pence per page. However, if you place the agreement on the left-hand side of an A4 sheet turned sideways and the child's record card (see page 52) on the right-hand side and photocopy this sheet, you can make a joint form for 10 pence. It is important, though, that both parent and childminder have a copy of the agreement.

An example of an agreement between parent and childminder is given opposite.

Child's record card

A typical registration form enrolling a child for playgroup or nursery is given in Chapter 5. This can easily double as a child's record card to be held by the childminder. To avoid retyping this form a pack of ten child's record forms can be obtained from the National Childminding Association for a small sum.

Registration of child with the Social Services Department of your local authority

Each child must be registered with Social Services. Since many referrals come from this department most children are already registered. A childminder must register the others, and inform Social Services when any leave.

Rates

Rates vary from area to area. Usually minders can charge a slightly higher rate if a child is taken for less than six hours a day.

For example, for a period of less than six hours with a Hampshire childminder the recommended hourly rate is £1.50 (1989/90). The weekly rate recommended by a certain London borough is £40. Gingerbread suggests that rates charged ought never to be less than 90 pence per hour for each child escalating to £1.30 per hour for anti-social hours. The standard rate can be varied according to the prosperity of the area, the individual parents, and the number and kind of meals provided. A childminder is self-employed so she can fix her own rate.

Keeping simple accounts

Keep a diary

Always keep a diary putting down the child's name and time of arrival and departure and the total number of hours under the appropriate day. Even if the child keeps to fixed times and the parent pays the same amount each week, it is still wise to keep the entries in your diary. If you are registered for more than one child, each child could be colour coded in your diary. At the end of each week you can add up the hours and work out the amounts. Again, do this even if the parent pays each day. If you buy a diary with a notes section, you can enter the weekly amount for each child and the totals in this section.

To boost her income a childminder can care for older children during the holidays and after school. This does not alter the number of pre-school children she can take, but she should not take on so many that she jeopardizes the care of her toddlers. Rates, conditions, and whether she delivers and collects to and from school can be fixed according to each family. Write down this information on the agreement between parent and childminder.

If a parent falls behind with daily dues or weekly charges, there are several ways a childminder can recover her money. The Social Services Department offers financial assistance to low income families, if they deem it necessary the child remains in the care of the minder. Telephone the Social Services Department and tell them about the particular case. Often a portion of the weekly charges will be paid if the parent can make up the difference. But if the parent can no longer pay for child care, perhaps because of a redundancy in the family or ill health, and Social Services cannot help, the childminder must ask the family not to send the child again and recover any money owed through the county court if necessary. Citizens' Advice Bureaux supply small claims forms. The Children's Legal Centre in London runs a free advice service on Monday to Friday from 2.00 pm to 5.00 pm. It will answer questions on most aspects of the law relating to children.

Using a different coloured pen write down the expenses incurred each day for which you have no receipts; for example, fares, telephone calls and stamps. Again place the weekly totals in the notes section. A percentage of your domestic overheads can be charged as expenses. At the end of each week allocate an amount for heating, hot water, rent and rates, and wear and tear on your home. Enter these figures in the notes section for the week. You could increase some of these amounts as the number of children increases. If you own your own home, you cannot write off part of your mortgage repayments as expenses.

Saving and storing receipts

Keep all your receipts. In addition to the entries in your diary, for which you have no receipts, keep the till receipts whenever you buy food, drinks, toys, stationery, etc. Store all the receipts in date order grouped together by month. Keep the milk receipts separate.

Free milk

Each child in your care can receive a third of a pint of milk a day free. Reclaim the money from the Department of Social Security. You can obtain a WF/DN 15 form from your pre-school adviser. Complete it and send it, together with your milk receipts and a record of the number of children attending each day, to the director of social services or social work for signature. A claim should be made once every three months. Any amount claimed for the period prior to registration will not be reimbursed. Always file your return as soon as each quarter ends. The Department of Social Security should supply you with dated forms bearing your code number.

Profits

Look in your diary at the end of each week and add up the total amount of fees taken for that week. Then subtract all your expenses to obtain the week's profit.

You could record this information in a loose-leaf binder using a page for each week followed at the end of each month by a plastic envelope holding all the receipts for that particular month. On each week's sheet draw up two columns: one headed income and the other headed expenditure. For example:

Income	**Expenditure**	
£75	Food	£20.55
Breakdown:	Toys/stationery	£ 5.35
Jane £25	Miscellaneous	£ 3.60
Jack £15	Wear and tear	£ 5.00
Fred £35	Rent and rates	£ 8.00
	Heating/lights	£ 7.00
£75.00		£49.50

Net profit is £75.00 - £49.50 = £25.50

At the end of the tax year add together the weekly profits to arrive at your annual profit. This figure is used by the Inland Revenue to determine how much tax you owe. On 6 April each year start a new file for your income and expenditure and your receipts.

If you wish to keep a more sophisticated set of accounts, including a cash book and a petty cash book, read Chapter 10 on keeping accounts for a nursery school or playgroup. A cash book/attendance register can be obtained from the National Childminding Association for £4 (1989/90).

Lone parents pay tax if their net profit is more than £84.14 per week or £4375 per year (1989/90). Net profit means benefit plus fees from childminding minus expenses. If you are claiming benefit, your pre-school adviser can help on how your earnings will affect your benefits, such as Income Support or Family Credit. The Department of Social Security runs a free telephone enquiry service called Freeline Social Security on 0800 666555.

Married women or single women pay tax if their net profit plus other income is more than £2785 per year or £53.56 per week (1989/90).

Any childminder whose net profit is more than £43 a week (1989/90) must pay National Insurance contributions. Read Chapter 10 for details on how to pay these contributions. *Tax and National Insurance Guide for Childminders* is updated annually by the National Childminding Association. It is sent out free to members.

Competition

Ring your local Social Services Department to find out how many childminders are registered in your immediate area and if there are any day nurseries or playgroups that might constitute competition. Look around to see if there is a demand for childminders. Attract parents by offering a better service. The best way to get children is by word of mouth recommendation. When a child leaves, for whatever reason, stay on good terms with the parents if at all possible. A childminder can advertise for children in the same way as a playgroup.

Prospects and support

Some Social Services Departments organise courses for childminders. There is often an initial course which is free, and runs one day a week for a few weeks. One-off courses are also often held on such topics as home safety or acquired immune deficiency syndrome (AIDS). Each region often has a few drop-in centres where childminders and their children can meet once a week. Check with your local pre-school adviser.

The National Childminding Association may also be able to help you develop your career. It will give advice on how to form a childminders' group. A booklet called *How to Start a Group* is available from the Association for a small charge. A more expensive study pack and training programme called *Childminding: Working with Children and Families* is available from the Community Education Development Centre. This pack was developed by the Open University and the National Childminding Association. It contains 22 topic leaflets, an introduction, and guide and group notes. The material has been designed to help childminders gain skills, build confidence, and see themselves as an important part of the child care network. Write to or telephone the Open University for a list of the other study packs available on family and school. These, however, are more expensive.

The PPA may also be of help and will supply a list of publications. Many are not expensive or are free to members. Membership details are given in Chapter 7.

If your childminding career takes off and you have a large enough home or can rent premises, it might be an idea to expand into a private playgroup. Mornings are often more popular than afternoons with parents or carers for the children who attend part time. Before embarking on such a project read *Starting a PPA Group* published by the PPA, and the relevant chapters in this book. Remember that you must reregister with Social Services if the nature of child care you offer changes.

Some childminders have taken Montessori classes in order to understand more about a child's pattern of development. Read Chapter 12 for more details of these and other courses.

Some local authorities advocate that under-twos ought not to attend day care establishments, which makes it necessary for them to be cared for in their own homes or those of childminders. Thus childminders are very much in demand; it is up to them to provide as good a service as possible. Social Services are promoting this facility positively.

Chapter 12

Courses

Once a private playgroup or nursery has registered with the Social Services Department of its local authority, there is often little guidance given on day-to-day running, provided the child to helper ratio is maintained and fire and safety precautions taken. This is good in one way, since there is no interference from Social Services, but the helpers and proprietors are left with the responsibility of offering a good facility to the general public. Some may be new to the child care network; others may have no qualifications as local authorities do not expect helpers to be trained for work in certain facilities.

For example, a proprietor of a new business may hire one or more unqualified helpers to minimise costs during the start-up period. But both the playgroup or nursery and the individual will benefit if these helpers complete a part-time course.

Take the mother of school age children who wishes to set up a playgroup. She could take one of the PPA foundation courses held in her area, putting her younger children, if any, in the creche organised by the course. (PPA courses run from September to June.) When the time comes to set up her own playgroup she will have this knowledge to help her. She could do a course while looking for premises. From starting the search for a church hall to the commencement of rental might easily take a year.

Another example is a businessman weighing up the pros and cons of installing a workplace nursery for his employees' children. Does he know any nursery nurses to help him set up such a facility? Should he consult his local college of higher education? This chapter may help him to decide.

There are many colleges that run courses which are useful, and often essential, to the helper working in an independent playgroup or nursery. Since one specific qualification may be a prerequisite for the job, it may help some prospective proprietors to decide upon the type of child care they wish to offer. For instance, a registered nursery school must employ at least one helper with a Certificate of Education in Nursery/Infant Teaching, a Montessori school one or more helpers trained in the

Montessori Method. A playgroup can operate with unqualified staff but it is unwise to do so.

Many local authorities suggest that a day nursery employs as many NNEBs as possible, nursery school teachers being a good alternative. A PPA foundation course attendance certificate rates highly for playgroup employees. The BTEC National Diploma in Caring Services (Nursery Nursing) is becoming increasingly popular. Proprietors who have been in the child care business for a few years might not be aware that more colleges are now running this BTEC course. A local college of education can be a useful source of trainee help and staff. The value of being on good terms with a local college cannot be underestimated.

Qualifications arising from social care, hospital play specialism, and children with special needs courses are often more popular with employees working in the state sector. More information on these and other courses can be gathered from the directories for students held in the reference section of your local library. For example, consult the current editions of *Directory of Further Education: CRAC* (published by Hobsons), *Higher Education in the United Kingdom: A Handbook for Students and their Advisers* (Longman) and *Colleges and Institutes of Higher Education Guide* (the Standing Conference of Principals). A free copy of the last can be obtained from the Standing Conference of Principals at Edge Hill College of Higher Education.

The Oxford Creche Development Project runs a creche development course which lasts for 12 weeks. Telephone for details. Many adult education centres run courses on child care, creche work, introduction to work with the under fives, supporting a child's learning, etc. Some local authorities publish this information in a brochure. For example, ILEA publishes annually *Floodlight: ILEA Guide to Part-time Day and Evening Classes in Inner London* available from major booksellers.

Social Services sometimes organise courses, so telephone the Social Services Department of your local authority for details.

Information about courses for those who wish to improve their business skills is given on page 148.

National Nursery Examination Board (NNEB) Certificate course

This qualification is recognised throughout the child care network. Those who hold it are called nursery nurses. The National Nursery Examination Board (NNEB) says that 'a qualified nursery nurse will understand the development of children from birth to the age of seven and will have the skills needed to care for them'.

The approved courses leading to the award of the NNEB last two years. Anyone who has passed school-leaving age by the beginning of the course may apply. Competition is often keen so, although most colleges stipulate no specific entry requirements, it is wise to have some practical experience, a good level of written and spoken English, and some O levels or CSE grade 1 passes (or the GCSE equivalent). Some colleges ask for two or more O levels or CSE grade 1 passes. The final certificate is awarded on academic work, practical work, and on obtaining a pass in two written examinations.

Many colleges run approved courses and will give information on courses, registration fees, entry requirements, selection procedures, etc if supplied with a stamped addressed envelope. Each college will have introduced its own variation but two-fifths of each course is spent working with children.

Course outline

- physical development of children from birth to seven
- education of children from birth to seven
- intellectual, emotional and social development of children from birth to seven
- child care
- cookery and nutrition
- safety and first aid
- the sick child
- health, immunity and infectious diseases
- the work of the health visitor, social worker, and Social Services.

Scottish Nursery Nurses' Board (SNNB) registration

This has replaced the Scottish Nursery Nurses' Examination Board certificate and became effective with the students who qualified in June 1986. The normal route to registration at the present time is a two-year full-time programme of education and training in all aspects of nursery nursing. The programme is offered in colleges of further education with practical training carried out in nursery schools/classes, infant departments in primary schools, day nurseries or children's/family centres.

Entry is open to those who have completed a four-year course of secondary education.

Scottish Vocational Education Council (SCOTVEC)

Scottish Vocational Education Council National Certificate modules Caring Group (Nursery Nurse Training) are available.

The Business and Technician Education Council (BTEC) National Diploma in Caring Services (Nursery Nursing)

Course outline

- human growth and development
- child care: practice and services
- first aid and safety
- learning activities and play including creative studies
- home environment studies including nutrition
- data interpretation and the social sciences
- science for education
- common skills assignment (A) and (B)
- community assignment
- sociological aspects of child development
- psychological aspects of child development
- early childhood education
- health education
- special needs
- child care: the sick child

An application must be made direct to the college of your choice but write first or telephone for a prospectus. The minimum entry requirements are four GCSE grade A, B or C; four GCE grade A, B or C; four CSE grade 1; appropriate CPVE; or BTEC First Course in Caring. Mature students with practical experience may also get a place despite having less than the entry requirements. The duration of the course is two years of full-time study or three years of part-time study. The course outlined above defined by BTEC is modified by each college to fit the needs of the area, the students and prospective employers. Students spend 500 to 800 hours on supervised work placements.

BTEC expects many more colleges to offer this qualification in the near future, as it has received so many enquiries from colleges. Until now only those running the NNEB course have run the BTEC course but this is expected to change. For more information contact BTEC Information Services. The NNEB and BTEC courses are both equally useful to the prospective nursery nurse.

State-funded nursery nurses college of further education courses

Only one state-funded nursery nurses college of further education, Bristol Nursery Nurses College, now remains. Of the 500 students enrolled

- 250 are studying for NNEB;
- 40 are studying for the Certificate of Post-qualifying Studies (CPQS);
- 30 are doing the Youth Training Scheme (YTS) Practical Course in Caring for Children in the Home.

The remainder are taking the special needs 'outset' course, hospital play specialist's course and foundation courses in care and management of children, etc. The three-year NNEB course is unique to this college. It is geared towards mature students from multicultural backgrounds with children, is part time, and involves short-day study. For a prospectus and more details of the courses available, write to the college enclosing a stamped addressed envelope.

Independent nursery training college courses

The following colleges offer courses in child care but most are residential:

Chiltern Nursery Training College, 16 Peppard Road, Caversham, Reading, Berkshire RG4 8JZ; 0734 471847/471131

Norland Nursery Training College, Denford Park, Hungerford, Berkshire RG17 0PQ 0488 82252

The Princess Christian College, 26 Wilbraham Road, Fallowfield, Manchester M14 6JX; 061-224 4560

The entry requirement for a place at one of these colleges is three GCSE grade A, B or C; three GCE grade A, B or C; or three CSE grade 1. The prospective student is expected to have a reasonable level of English and one of the above examinations must be in English language. She must be at least 18 years of age.

Each college has a day care unit and a nursery school. Students spend time in these and other child care facilities.

Chiltern Nursery Training College courses
Students are coached for the award of the NNEB and the Royal Society of Health Diploma of Nursery Nursing. Fees are high. It is unlikely that a grant can be obtained but a small number of bursaries are available. Anyone interested should write or telephone the college, and ask for a syllabus and prospectus. Twenty students are admitted in January and 30 in September.

Chiltern Nursery Training College has introduced a one-year Practical Child Care course for which a certificate is awarded upon successful completion. There are a small number of non-residential as well as residential places. The principal said when she announced the course that she hopes the outcome 'will be a small but a growing band of people who are better equipped to work in the ever-increasing field of childminding, playgroups, creches, etc'.

Norland Nursery Training College courses
During the course students are prepared for the award of the NNEB and the Royal Society of Health Diploma of Nursery Nursing, the Norland Preliminary Certificate and the Norland Diploma and Badge. Fees are high and the uniform is a costly addition. The Maiden Scheme, however, accepts students at 17 years of age to help in the dining room and with light domestic duties for a period of 12 months. If they prove satisfactory, the full training fees are halved and a grant is given towards the cost of the first uniform. New students can start in January and September each year. Write for a prospectus and more details of the Maiden Scheme enclosing a stamped addressed envelope.

The Princess Christian College courses
This college offers a training in child care and nursery management. It prepares students for the award of the NNEB, the Royal Society of Health Diploma of Nursery Nursing and the Princess Christian Certificate. Again, the fees are high and a grant is unlikely.

Privately trained nursery nurses (for example, Norland nannies) are unlikely to seek work in a playgroup or nursery since they can often earn more working for families. Those who wish to further their career might be persuaded, so might a nanny who is thinking of running her own playgroup, nursery or day nursery. Some nannies, having been on call day and night intermittently perhaps for several years, may find a 8.30 am to 4.00 pm job appealing.

Pre-school Playgroups Association (PPA) courses

There are 422 branches of the Pre-school Playgroups Association (PPA) which place an emphasis on play and the development of the child within the family and in the playgroup. The PPA runs a foundation course and an advanced course for those interested in under-fives; advice on how to set up and run a playgroup is given. It also runs a fieldworkers' course. A certificate of assessment is awarded on completion of each course. For example, a student must complete 120 hours of the foundation course to pass. Courses are held at adult education centres on one day a week and last for one year. Fees are not high. For more details contact the PPA National Centre between 8.45 am and 5.00 pm during the week, or write. These qualifications are not recognised nationally but they are considered to be useful for staff with no other child care training. This view is held by many local authorities.

London Montessori Centre courses

Montessori nursery teaching qualifications are awarded by the London Montessori Centre. It runs a Nursery (Foundation) Teaching Diploma course and an NNEB Certificate and Child Care Diploma course. Both are full time and fees are over £800 per term. The part-time courses are less expensive but only the Nursery (Foundation) Teaching Diploma can be studied in this way. Fees are £250 per term. The Nursery (Foundation) Teaching Diploma can also be awarded as part of a tutor-guided correspondence course. Fees are £255 and include a registration fee of £110. All fees include course books and textbooks but workshop and examination fees are additional. It is possible to pay in instalments. Reductions are sometimes given to playgroup leaders.

Nursery (Foundation) Teaching Diploma

This course is necessary for an understanding of the Montessori philosophy and is suitable for students wishing to teach Montessori Method to two-and-a-half to seven year olds. The syllabus includes Montessori philosophy, child development, Montessori exercises of practical life, sensorial apparatus, mathematics apparatus, language skills and Montessori reading materials, environmental studies, children's literature, art, music, movement and the preparation of Montessori reference files. The full-time course also covers philosophy, sociology and psychology of education, curriculum studies, observation techniques, school management, and teaching skills including 200 hours of teaching practice. This longer course will probably be of more use to those running or wishing to start up a Montessori nursery school.

NNEB and Child Care and Teaching Diploma
NNEB students attend additional lectures on the Montessori Method and spend time working in hospitals, day care centres, families, assessment centres and homes for children with special needs. This is a useful course for those who can spare the time and the money. It allows the successful student to work in any type of nursery school.

Montessori workshops

These workshops are held by the London Montessori Centre for students and anyone else concerned with child welfare and education. Montessori apparatus is demonstrated, so students obtain practical experience. These workshops should help those running schools, and teachers, nannies and childminders, etc.

In addition to this centre, there is St Nicholas Montessori College based in London and the Irish Montessori Centre in Dublin. There are also centres overseas.

St Nicholas Montessori College courses

St Nicholas Montessori College in London qualifies students to work in the Montessori system. It runs full-time diploma courses, part-time diploma courses, and external diploma courses and workshops. Fees range from £200 to £2200 per course. The courses at each level have four main aims:

- a thorough understanding of the Montessori educational philosophies, as well as those of current educationists;
- an understanding of child psychology;
- a familiarity with the Montessori teaching/didactic materials;
- a thorough grounding in all subjects needed to teach children in nursery and infant schools.

It publishes a useful leaflet called *How to Start a Montessori Class.*

Registered General Nurse (RGN) and Registered Sick Children's Nurse (RSCN)

Both these qualifications are useful to those working in a nursery or creche. Many day nurseries and creches that take children under three years of age may have a nurse on their payroll. This helps to reassure parents of very young children, who are separated for most of the day.

Certificate of Education in Nursery Teaching and Certificate of Education in Infant Teaching

These qualifications are useful and necessary for those working in or setting up and running a nursery school.

Correspondence courses

Montessori correspondence courses have been mentioned previously (see page 146). International Correspondence Schools Limited (ICS) has offices in Sutton, Glasgow and London. It offers a course in child day care. This course concentrates on children from birth to the age of eight, including topics such as health, safety and nutrition, development through play, and child care facilities. A free child care kit is issued to each student. ICS also gives advice on how to start your own playgroup or nursery or embark upon a career of childminding. An ICS Diploma is awarded upon completion of the course. The fees for this course, however, are over £200.

Open University courses

Write to the Open University enclosing a stamped addressed envelope for details of courses on child care, business and small business.

Business Courses

Consult your local Chamber of Commerce, business resource centre and job training scheme for information on small business courses in your region. Head Start, Project Fullemploy and Joblink may also be able to help.

BTEC training for small firms

BTEC offers nine courses to those from small firms from Raising

Finance for the Small Firm to Management and Leadership within the Small Firm. It helps those employed in running their own small business or those about to set up one to develop the skills required to run a small firm; training is based on each individual's needs.

BTEC first courses

These courses cater for people in work as well as for those preparing for employment. The qualifications are recognised nationally. Subjects such as business and finance, computing and information systems, information technology, management, and caring services would be useful to those working in or setting up a playgroup or nursery. These courses are held in colleges, polytechnics and schools throughout the country.

ICS runs correspondence courses such as Running Your Own Business, Business Management, and Book-keeping and Accountancy. Your local small firms bureau may know of other courses. Read the small business pages in the national press. Good books and courses on small business are often mentioned. The days on which to watch out for these columns are:

Mondays in the *Guardian*
Tuesdays, New Business in the *Financial Times*
Fridays, Your Own Business in *The Times*, the *Independent*, and the *Daily Telegraph*

Family money is dealt with on Saturdays by most of these papers.

Chapter 13

'How I Started'

Cromwell Creche
10–12 Pennant Mews, London W8

The Cromwell Hospital is a private hospital. The creche is an autonomous hospital department, and it began in a self-contained suite of rooms in the main hospital building. It moved over to the mews once conversion work was completed. The number of children had grown rapidly. The creche was originally intended for the sole use of hospital employees. However, during the appeal against the Planning Department of the Royal Borough of Kensington and Chelsea (who were against the change of use of premises from residential to creche) local residents were so supportive that it was decided to offer 50 per cent of the places to residents' children.

The creche is open 52 weeks of the year from 9.00am to 5.00pm Monday to Friday including bank holidays. Extended hours operate for hospital staff and for other parents who might need this facility. Fees are £70 per week (1988/89) with two free weeks a year to allow for holiday arrangements. Staff fees are subsidised by the hospital. The creche is licensed for children from the ages of 6 weeks to five years. Because of the demand for places for young babies, the older children are encouraged to leave at four years to spend a year at nursery school before going to 'big' school. There are now 22 children on the register who are looked after by four nursery nurses (NNEBs) and two helpers.

Outlined below is a rough programme of the children's day in the creche.

7.45 am - 9.00 am	Children arrive. Breakfast for some.
9.00 am - 10.00 am	Time spent with constructive toys, puzzles, games, nursery rhymes. Change and toilet.
10.00 am - 10.30 am	Toast and milk.
10.30 am - 10.45 am	Playbus.
10.45 am - 11.45 am	Group out for walk. Others - general activities using larger equipment and toys. Wendy house.

11.45 am -12 noon	Change and toilet.
12 noon - 1.00 pm	Lunch.
1.00 pm - 2.00 pm	Rest. Story. Change and toilet.
2.00 pm - 3.30 pm	Sand and water, painting, slide, craftwork, music, cooking.
3.30 pm - 4.00 pm	Tea.
4.00 pm - 6.00 pm	Change and toilet. Cars, bikes, trains, dolls house. Group story telling. Children go home.

A hot two-course lunch is served to the children daily. This is cooked in the hospital restaurant; it is collected by one of the creche staff at 11.45 am. This means that no actual cooking has to be done in the creche; the kitchen is only used for milk feeds and the making of breakfast and tea. Pureed food and cereals are provided by the mothers of younger babies, as are disposable nappies.

Older brothers and sisters can spend entire school holidays, half term, or just the occasional day at creche if the numbers allow and if the parents require it.

The Apples Nursery School
Hatt Common, Ball Hill, Near Newbury, Berkshire

Caroline Cox and her sister Sally Goble are joint proprietors of the Apples Nursery School. It is set in a small village six miles from Newbury. They offer sessional care to 60 children during term time. Children can attend from 9.00 am to 12.30 pm and from 12.00 pm to 3.00 pm but some children stay for the whole day. The fees are £9.00 for a full day or £5 for a session (1988/89).

The emphasis is on educational development. Many parents send their children to the Apples to learn first to play and to develop their motor skills, and then to progress to phonetic and number work. Some children are ready to learn to read before they leave. The children sit between 9.00 am and 10.30 am and do their work. There is a good selection of writing books - some hand made and others bought from Early Learning Centre. This is followed by directive play. Then children staying all day eat their packed lunches and sleep for a short time. During the changeover period from morning to afternoon session educational videos are shown. The pattern of the afternoon session is similar to that of the morning. This nursery school is of a particularly high standard; the proprietors know the head teachers of the local schools and are very interested in pre-school and primary education.

Working parents use this facility; however, they usually work part time and do not require full-time child care. Caroline says that some children are collected by childminders but she must know exactly in advance who, other than the parents, is entitled to pick up or deliver a child.

This small private nursery school was opened in September 1987. Caroline was already working in a private nursery which was about to close, so she was looking around for premises for her own venture. A farm shop came up for sale, and this pushed Caroline and Sally into action. They managed to acquire the freehold at the end of June, and held an open day at the end of the summer term. Registration forms were available on the open day, and many families registered their children. The registration fee of £5 did not deter them. Caroline also took 12 children with her from her previous job so the nursery school was committed to opening its doors at the beginning of the next term. Most things had to be sorted out during the summer holidays. Caroline says that this was probably the worst time of year, but they managed it. Fire regulations were complied with and planning permission for change of use was obtained, registration with the Social Services Department of Hampshire County Council was effected and insurance was taken out. Two NNEBs and one part-time helper were hired to help Caroline who has a Certificate of Education, specialising in nursery education.

In addition, the free services of both husbands were exploited. Caroline's husband, an architect, drew up the plans, and Sally's husband, an accountant, arranged the insurance and gave them sound financial advice. Both husbands helped with painting. Sally is the full-time administrator, doing all the books, paying the bills and the salaries, and she sometimes works in the nursery.

Sally said that setting up was an exhausting period. Each household's telephone bills were unusually large. She found Berkshire County Council very helpful. They even allowed her to submit a tender for some second-hand tables and small chairs which was accepted. She uses the services of a carpenter to custom-build some things, such as bookcases, and to mend others. The parents donated toys and goods that they no longer wanted. Sally and Caroline brought in many things from their own homes.

Caroline does a small amount of fund raising by selling Apples T-shirts and sweatshirts and running raffles. Sally has set up a special bank account for the purchase of a slide which is the current fund-raising project. Sally says that her staff have been very loyal and have worked unpaid overtime. She plans to reward them when the first year's accounts have been compiled. Places are booked for the next two years at least; some babies have their names on the waiting list. So far the venture is a complete success.

Pooh Corner Montessori Nursery School Christchurch, Victoria Road, London W8

Sally-Anne Greville-Heygate, once a photographer, now runs and owns Pooh Corner Montessori Nursery School in London. Having worked in the nursery herself for eight years, she bought it in 1985. Since the nursery does not own its own premises, a church hall, she gained the right to continue with the rental, all the equipment, goodwill and the waiting list. The initial start-up money came from Sally-Anne's savings and a fixed interest business loan from the National Westminster Bank. She based the amount of the loan on fees generated and expenses incurred (including repayment of the loan) over a period of four years. The business has reached break-even point (it has never lost money) and, once the loan is repaid, a profit is predicted.

Pooh Corner is registered with the Social Services Department of the Royal Borough of Kensington and Chelsea for 19 children. Children can attend between the ages of two-and-a-half and five years. The younger ones attend the afternoon sessions from 1.30 pm to 3.30 pm Monday to Thursday, and the older children attend each weekday morning from 9.15 am to 12.30 pm. Sally-Anne, a trained Montessori teacher with a full-time teaching diploma, works full time in the nursery alongside Penelope James. Penelope, a qualified NNEB, has also completed a part-time course at St Nicholas Training Centre for the Montessori Method of Education which led to a Montessori Teaching Diploma. Sally-Anne paid her fees and allowed her time off for study. Students from the London Montessori Centre and St Nicholas Montessori Centre are sometimes placed at Pooh Corner to gain teacher training experience.

The afternoon class is limited to ten children. The children are encouraged to learn to share, develop hand control, and to start to gain both concentration and self-discipline. The morning class, of up to 19 children, is more structured. Skills acquired during the afternoon session are reinforced. Sandpaper letters and numbers are introduced, and the alphabet is taught phonetically. Sally-Anne says that by five most children are able to read and write three- and four-letter words; phonograms are introduced, and they can do simple addition and subtraction up to 20. Paint and playdo are put out during every session. Sally-Anne saves money by making her own playdough. She watches *Blue Peter* to get new ideas for things to make. She always keeps a copy of everything made for reference. One child will usually be asked to make the file copy. Each child's work is kept in a file, and they take their work home once a week. There is usually a project for the week. This term's projects include dinosaurs, art appreciation, the structure of an orchestra and the Spanish Armada. An exhibition of the children's work is staged at the end of each term, and the children take part in summer and Christmas plays. A ballet teacher is paid £12 for a 45-minute session to teach ballet once a week. This is enjoyed by both boys and girls. There is a church garden where the children can play during fine weather. It is well equipped with a sandpit, pushalongs and a trampoline.

Pooh Corner is closed during the holidays. Fees are paid termly in advance. A £75 deposit is held against children leaving unexpectedly at the end of term. One term's notice ensures that the £75 deposit is deducted from the last term's fees. Children who attend the morning class pay £340 per term, and those who have a place in the afternoons pay £240 (1988/89). Fees are the only source of income. Preference is given to children who live in the area and those whose brothers or sisters have already attended Pooh Corner. There are about 20 names for each term on the waiting list. Children are allocated places during the term before they are due to begin. Pooh Corner is on the Under-Fives Sheet of ISIS and on the Child Care Sheet sent out by the Social Services Department of the Royal Borough of Kensington and Chelsea. No other advertising is placed; Sally-Anne relies very much on recommendations by word of mouth.

Pooh Corner is unable to expand because of lack of space, and Sally-Anne feels that it is an ideal size to maintain an intimate and trusting relationship between children, staff and parents.

Bridgewater Square Nursery
1 Bridgewater Square, London EC2

Lynn Beck and Tilly Hamilton run a workplace nursery for Merrill Lynch. Despite its status as a voluntary organisation it is included here as it is a good example of a workplace nursery.

City Child is open from 8.30 am until 6.00 pm. There are 22 children on the register but the nursery is registered for 30. There are six babies under the age of 18 months, and there is one NNEB to two babies. Ten NNEBs, one state-enrolled nurse (SEN), and one cook are on the payroll. The cleaning is done by an outside contractor. Tilly is the coordinator and Lynn is the assistant coordinator. Two members of staff are doing part-time Montessori courses. They work in the nursery.

The nursery has 3000 square feet of space and a large garden which is completely fenced in. There is a public swimming pool opposite. Children are taken swimming once a week, usually in a group of two or three accompanied by staff. The indoor space is divided into a quiet room which is used for floor-based activities and has a home corner. This room doubles as the sleeping room in the afternoon. Sleeping bags and mattresses are provided. Each child's belongings are denoted by a symbol such as a circle, a square or a triangle and children as young as 18 months can identify their own symbols. There is a messy room with an easily washable floor where paints, clay and paste are used. Each baby has a cot in the nursery adjoining the baby kitchen and laundry. Mothers are asked to supply nappies for those children who are not potty trained but all food and drink are provided. There are five children's toilets, one disabled toilet and two staff toilets.

Leading off the staff room there is a large kitchen where the cook prepares the meals. Lunch is usually a ready prepared main course from Elmdale Foods served with fresh vegetables and home-made pudding. Lynn sometimes cooks the main course, certainly all the vegetarian food, but she has found that the children like the ready prepared meals and they are easier since a batch of meals is delivered once every eight weeks. The favourites are fish in sauce, bolognaise, hot pot, macaroni cheese and the dishes with sauces. Deciding on the menu has been a matter of trial and error; some foods have proved to be too salty for the children. The kitchen is well equipped with a caterers' fridge and dishwasher. Lunch is served at 11.45 am, and a high tea at 3.15 pm. The remainder of the shopping is done weekly at Safeway when one NNEB will take some children with her.

The remaining room is large and the children meet there in the morning and breakfast together. It is used throughout the day for many activities such as Duplo and dressing up.

Tilly helped to set up this facility, working a couple of months on her own before it opened in January 1988. The organisation City Child has been in operation for ten years. Its aim is to provide more child care in the City of London as the City has very few registered childminders. Start-up funds were raised by City institutions, and when the developers London Metropolitan were building new offices for Merrill Lynch, Islington Council stipulated that to obtain planning permission they must supply a 30-place workplace nursery. Eventually the site in the Barbican was found, and a ten-year lease was rented. Tilly was given a £21,000 grant for the first six months. All the building and decorating work was done and paid for before they moved in. But then with the help of the committee Tilly and Lynn had to equip the entire nursery from cots to kitchen equipment. Tilly has worked out that the fees generated by 26 children ought to allow the nursery to reach break-even point. Parents pay £415 for each child per calendar month (1988/89). Norwich Union has now taken over the funding, and they will cover any losses.

Employees of Merrill Lynch have first call on places, and the company gives a two-thirds subsidy. This subsidy is extended to fathers as well as mothers. Other children are taken, and the only requirement is that their parents live or work within the City of London. Tilly's biggest monthly bill is the salaries. She pays the NNEBs between £7500 and £9600 per annum (1988/89). She pays for insurance, food, rates and equipment but the inclusive rent is taken care of.

Both Tilly and Lynn said that setting up involved a lot of hard work. The Social Services Department of the City of London were very helpful although strict requirements had to be met. Extra locks were required before the insurance could be taken out, and there was an inspection by the Fire Officer. Much of the equipment has been bought from major nursery/playgroup suppliers such as Galt, and Tilly said that John Lewis had supplied them with a trade card and offered free delivery of goods.

Mothers or fathers are encouraged to telephone the nursery during the day if they are worried about their children, and are allowed to visit during the day; for example, during their lunch break. They are expected to help to settle their child initially. Tilly and all her staff try to accommodate the parents' wishes at all times. She thinks it is very important to have a good working relationship with the parents. If a child becomes ill the parents are telephoned immediately, and kept informed of the child's progress throughout the day.

This is an ideal facility for those who wish to remain in full-time employment after the birth of a child. Fees are high but with an employer's subsidy seem almost bearable, despite the fact that the employee has to pay tax on this subsidy.

Chapter 14

Addresses

Acorn (Percussion) Ltd
Unit 34, Abbey Business Centre, London SW8 3NS; 01-720 2243

Action GT Ltd
Brook House, Duke Street, Henley-on-Thames, Oxfordshire RG9 1UP; 0491 572406

Adam Leisure Ltd
Adam House, Ripon Way, Harrogate, Yorkshire HG1 2AU; 0423 501151

Advisory, Conciliation and Arbitration Service (ACAS)
Head Office: 27 Wilton Street, London SW1X 7AZ; 01-210 3600; for regional offices, see telephone book

Allan Industries
Coronation Road, High Wycombe, Buckinghamshire HP12 3RR; 0494 35041

Alliance of Small Firms & Self Employed People
33 The Green, Calne, Wiltshire SN11 8DJ; 0249 817003

Ambi (Kebrico)
Unit 8, Whorlton Road, Riverside Park Industrial Estate, Middlesbrough, Cleveland TS2 1QT; 0642 240553

Appletree Leisure Ltd
Watnall Road, Hucknall, Nottingham NG15 6ET; 0602 635222

Association Montessori Internationale
Maria Montessori Training Organisation, 26 Lyndhurst Gardens, London NW3 5NW; 01-435 3646

Association of British Insurers
Aldermary House, 10–15 Queen Street, London EC4N 1TT; 01-248 4477

Association of Independent Businesses
Trowbray House, 108 Weston Street, London SE1 3QB; 01-403 4066

Association of Nursery Training Colleges *see* page 144, Princess Christian College.

Atlascraft
17 Ludlow Hill Road, West Bridgford, Nottingham NG2 6HD; 0602 23451

Bambola Toys Ltd
Tresham Works, Kettering, Northamptonshire NN16 8SB; 0536 81881

Bandia UK Ltd
Steward House, Sydenham Road, Guildford, Surrey GU1 3SR; 0483 63311

Bendy Toys Ltd
Ashford Road, Ashford, Middlesex TW15 1XH; 07842 42001

Beimme
Watnall Road, Hucknall, Nottingham NG15 6ET; 0602 635222

Big Box Ltd
11 Pembroke Mews, London W8 6ER; 01-938 2594

Blue Arrow Personnel Services Ltd
123-7 Cannon Street, London EC4N 5AX; 01-626 9621

Bontempi UK Ltd
Brennard Mill, Fraser Street, Burnley, Lancashire BB10 1UL; 0282 35431

Britains Petite Ltd
Blackhorse Lane, London E17 5QD; 01-527 0041

British Association for Early Childhood Education (BAECE)
Studio 3/2, 140 Tabernacle Street, London EC2A 4SD; 01-250 1768

British Institute of Management
Management House, Cottingham Road, Corby, Northamptonshire NN17 1TT; 0536 204222

British Insurance Brokers' Association
BIBA House, 14 Bevis Marks, London EC3A 7NT; 01-623 9043

The British Nutrition Foundation
15 Belgrave Square, London SW1X 8PS; 01-235 4904

British Red Cross Society
National Headquarters, 9 Grosvenor Crescent, London SW1X 7EJ; 01-235 5454

British Safety Council
62 Chancellors Road, London W6 9RS; 01-741 1231

British Standards Institution
2 Park Street, London W1A 2BS; 01-629 9000

British Toys and Hobbies Association
80 Camberwell Road, London SE5 0EG; 01-701 7271

British Venture Capital Association
24 Upper Brook Street, London W1Y 1PD; 01-836 5702

Builders Merchants Federation
15 Soho Square, London W1V 5FB; 01-439 1753

Building Employers Confederation
82 New Cavendish Street, London W1M 8AD; 01-580 5588

Business and Technician Education Council (BTEC)
Information Services, Central House, Upper Woburn Place, London WC1H 0HH; 01-388 3288

Business Expansion Scheme (BES) *see* Local Investment Networking Company

Business in the Community
227a City Road, London EC1V 1LX; 01-253 3716

Business Resource Centre
9 Thorpe Close, Ladbroke Grove, London W10 5XL; 01-969 9455

Caesarcraft
Ryalls Lane, Cambridge, Gloucestershire GL2 7AT; 045389 394

Cassidy Bros (Casdon)
Casdon Works, Mitcham Road, Blackpool FY4 4QW; 0253 66411

Charity Commission
London: St Alban's House, 57-60 Haymarket, London SW1Y 4QX; 01-210 3000
Northern: Graeme House, Derby Square, Liverpool L2 7SB; 051-227 3191

Chartered Association of Certified Accountants
29 Lincoln's Inn Fields, London WC2A 3EE; 01-242 6855

Chicco
Watnall Road, Hucknall, Nottingham NG15 6ET; 0602 635222

Child Accident Prevention Trust
28 Portland Place, London W1N 4DE; 01-636 2545

The Children's Legal Centre Ltd
20 Compton Terrace, London N1 2UN; 01-359 6251

The Children's Society
Edward Rudolf House, 69-85 Margery Street, London WC1X 0JL; 01-837 4299

Childsplay
112 Tooting High Street, London SW17 0RR; 01-672 6470

City and Guilds of London Institute
76 Portland Place, London W1N 4AA; 01-580 3050

Commission of the European Communities
8 Storey's Gate, London SW1P 3AT; 01-222 8122

Community Education Development Centre (CEDC)
Briton Road, Coventry CV2 4LF; 0203 440814

Community Playthings
Robertsbridge, East Sussex TN32 5DR; 0580 880626

Companies Registration Office
England and Wales: Companies House, Crown Way, Maindy, Cardiff CF4 3UZ; 0222 388588
Scotland: 102 George Street, Edinburgh EH2 3DJ; 031-225 5774
Northern Ireland: Department of Economic Development, 64

Chichester Street, Belfast BT1 4JX; 0232 234488

Confederation for the Registration of Gas Installers (CORGI)
St Martin's House, 140 Tottenham Court Road, London W1P 0AS

Consumers' Association
2 Marylebone Road, London NW1 4DX; 01-839 1222

The Co-operative Development Agency
21 Panton Street, London SW1Y 4DR; 01-839 2988

Corgi Sales Ltd
Kingsway, Swansea Industrial Estate, Fforestfach, Swansea SA5 4EL; 0792 586223

Council for Small Industries in Rural Areas (CoSIRA) *See* Rural Development Commission. Local branches are listed in telephone books, possibly still under CoSIRA.

Crayola (Binney & Smith Ltd)
Ampthill Road, Bedford, Bedfordshire MK42 9RS; 0234 60201

Customs & Excise Department
New King's Beam House, 22 Upper Ground, London SE1 9PS; 01-626 1313; *see also* Customs & Excise (Enquiries VAT) in your local telephone book

The Department of the Environment
2 Marsham Street, London SW1P 3EB; 01-212 3434; *see also* Environment in your local telephone book

Department of Health and **Department of Social Security**
see Health and Social Security in your local telephone book

The Department of Trade and Industry
1–19 Victoria Street, London SW1; 01-215 7877; *see also* Trade & Industry in your local telephone book

Early Learning Centre
Shop from your nearest branch or from Early Learning Centre, Hawksworth, Swindon, Wiltshire SN2 1TT; 0793 610171

Educa J T I Ltd
22–24 Plymouth Road, Tavistock, Devon PL19 9QN; 0822 5200

Educational Video Workshop
51 Crouch Hall Road, London N8 8HH; 01-348 2469

Ed-U-Games
20 Linden Terrace, Newton Abbot, Devon TQ12 1LL; 0626 69833

Edu-Play
450 Hinckley Road, Leicester; 0533 857849

English Estates
St George's House, Kingsway, Team Valley, Gateshead, Tyne and Wear NE11 0NA; 091-487 8941

English Heritage
Publications Branch, 23 Savile Row, London W1X 2HE; 01-734 6010

Enterprise Allowance Scheme *see* Jobcentres under Training Agency or Manpower Services Commission in your local telephone book

Equal Opportunities Commission
Policy Unit, Overseas House, Quay Street, Manchester M3 3HN; 061-833 9244

Escor Toys Ltd
Groveley Road, Christchurch, Dorset BH23 3RQ; 0202 485834

Federation of Employment Services
10 Belgrave Square, London SW1X 8PH, 01-235 6616

Federation of Master Builders
Headquarters, 33 John Street, London WC1N 2AT; 01-242 7583

FIMBRA
22 Great Tower Street, London EC3R 5AQ; 01-929 2711

Fire for administrative calls and enquiries *see* Fire in your local telephone book

Fisher Price Ltd
Monks Mead House, Bath Road, Hare Hatch, Reading, Berkshire RG10 9SA; 073522 4481

James Galt & Co Ltd
Brookfield Road, Cheadle, Cheshire SK8 2PN; 061-428 8511

George Luck
12 Gaston Lane, Martock, Somerset TA12 6LN; 0935 822743

Gingerbread
35 Wellington Street, London WC2E 7BN; 01-240 0953

Hamleys
188–196 Regent Street, London W1R 6BT; 01-734 3161

Hanbury Guest House
1 Hanbury Terrace, Barton Road, Tewkesbury, Gloucestershire GL20 5QH; 0684 299911

Hasbro Industries (UK) Ltd
Eskdale Road, Winnersh Triangle, Wokingham, Berkshire RG11 5LW; 0734 698514

Head Start
The Industrial Society, Peter Runge House, 3 Carlton House Terrace, London SW1Y 5DG; 01-839 4300

Health Education Authority
Hamilton House, Mabledon Place, London WC1H 9AJ; 01-631 0930

Health Education Council *see* Health Education Authority

Hestair Hope Ltd
St Philip's Drive, Royton, Oldham, Lancashire OL2 6AG; 061-652 1411

Highlands and Islands Development Board
Bridge House, 27 Bank Street, Inverness IV1 1QR; 0463 234171

Hiron Games
5 Hillgate Street, London W8 7SP; 01-229 9516

Home Start Consultancy
22 Princess Road West, Leicester LE1 6TP; 0533 554988

The Housing Corporation
149 Tottenham Court Road, London W1P 0BN; 01-387 9466

Hungry Owl
5 Charlotte Place, Off Uphill Drive, London NW9 0BU; 01-204 0143

Huntercraft
4 The Castle House, Sherborne, Dorset; 0935 812288

Independent Schools Information Service (ISIS) (Under-Fives sheets for London and South East only)
3 Vandon Street, London SW1H 0AN; 01-222 7274

Inland Revenue New Employers Starter Pack *see* Inland Revenue in your local telephone book

Instant Muscle
Haymill Centre, 112 Burnham Lane, Burnham, Slough SL1 6LZ; 06286 63926

Institute of Chartered Accountants in England and Wales
Chartered Accountants Hall, PO Box 433, Moorgate Place, London EC2P 2BJ; 01 628 7060

Institute of Chartered Accountants of Scotland
27 Queen Street, Edinburgh EH2 1LA; 031-225 5673

Institute of Plumbing
64 Station Lane, Hornchurch, Essex RM12 6MB

International Correspondence Schools Ltd (ICS)
England and Wales: 312–314 High Street, Sutton, Surrey SM1 1PR; 01-643 9568
Southern Ireland: 36 Hillcourt Road, Glenageary, Dun Laoghaire, County Dublin; 0001 853472
Scotland: Intertext House, 8 Elliot Place, Clydeway Centre, Glasgow G3 8EF; 041-221 2926

Job Creation Ltd
139A New Bond Street, London W1X 9FB; 01-409 2229

Jump
27 Cowper Street, London EC2A 4AP

Kiddicraft
Aztex West, Park Avenue, Bristol, BS12 4RF; 0454 616005

The Law Society
113 Chancery Lane, London WC2A 1PL; 01-242 1222

Lego UK Ltd
Ruthin Road, Wrexham, Clwyd LL13 7TQ; 0978 266949

Little Tikes Co
Technology House, Easthampstead Road, Bracknell, Berkshire RG12 1LX; 0344 411410

Living & Learning
32A Bridge Street, Cambridge CB2 1UJ; 0223 65445

The Local Enterprise Development Unit (LEDU)
LEDU House, Upper Galwally, Belfast BT8 4TB; 0232 691031

Local Investment Networking Company
4 Snow Hill, London EC1A 2DL; 01-236 3000

London Food Commission
88 Old Street, London EC1V 9AR; 01-235 9513

London Montessori Centre
18 Balderton Street, London W1Y 1TG; 01-493 0165

Manpower Services Commission *see* Training Agency

Matchbox Toys
240 Lincoln Road, Enfield, Middlesex EN1 1SP; 01-805 4567

Maternity Alliance
15 Britannia Street, London WC1X 9JP; 01-837 1265

Mattel UK Ltd
Meridian West, Leicester LE3 2WT; 0533 826666

Meccano
17 Ludlow Hill Road, West Bridgford, Nottingham NG2 6HD; 0602 23451

MENCAP *see* Royal Society for Mentally Handicapped Children

Merit Toys Ltd
Merit House, Cranbourne Road, Potters Bar, Hertfordshire EN6 3JY; 0707 57211

Michael Stanfield
Murdock Road, Bicester, Oxfordshire OX6 7RH; 0869 245071

Milton Bradley/Playskool
Spencer House, 23 Sheen Road, Richmond-on-Thames, Middlesex TW9 1AL; 01-940 6069

MIND *see* National Association for Mental Health

The Ministry of Agriculture, Fisheries and Food
Great Westminster House, Horseferry Road, London SW1P 2AE; 01-216 6311; *see also* Agriculture, Fisheries and Food in your local telephone book

The Missing Link Trading Co Ltd
38 Kendal Street, London W2 2BU, 01-262 2630

Montessori Association of Teachers and Schools (MATS)
18 Balderton Street, London W1Y 1TG; 01-629 7808

Montessori Equipment Company Ltd
Registrars Department, 18 Balderton Street, London W1Y 1TG; 01-493 0165

The Maria Montessori Training Organisation
26 Lyndhurst Gardens, London NW3 5NW; 01-435 3646

Musicland
39–45 Cold Harbour Lane, London SE5 9NR; 01-737 1245

National and Local Government Officers' Association (NALGO)
1 Mabledon Place, London WC1H 9AJ; 01-388 2366

National Association for Maternal and Child Welfare
1 South Audley Street, London W1Y 6JS; 01-491 1315

National Association for Mental Health (MIND)
22 Harley Street, London W1N 2ED; 01-637 0741

National Association for the Welfare of Children in Hospital (NAWCH)
Argyle House, 29–31 Euston Road, London NW1 2SD; 01-833 2041

National Association of Certificated Nursery Nurses (NACNN)
10 Meriden Court, Great Clacton, Essex CO15 4XH

National Association of Citizens' Advice Bureaux
115–123 Pentonville Road, London N1 9LZ; 01-833 2181

National Childbirth Trust (NCT)
9 Queensborough Terrace, London W2 3TB; 01-221 3833

National Childcare Campaign Ltd/Daycare Trust
Wesley House, 4 Wild Court, 70 Great Queen Street, London WC2B 5AU; 01-405 5617/5618

National Childminding Association
8 Mason's Hill, Bromley, Kent BR2 9EY; 01-464 6164

National Children's Bureau
8 Wakley Street, London EC1V 7QE; 01-278 9441

National Council of Voluntary Child Care Organisations (Childcare) (NCVCCO)
UFI (Childcare), 8 Wakley Street, London EC1V 7QE; 01-833 3319

National Council for Voluntary Youth Services
Wellington House, 29 Albion Street, Leicester LE1 6GD; 0533 471400

The National Federation of Self-employed and Small Businesses Ltd
32 St Anne's Road, West Lytham, St Annes, Lancashire FY8 1NY; 0253 720911

National Institute of Adult Education
19B De Montfort Street, Leicester LE1 7GE; 0533 551451

National Nursery Examination Board (NNEB)
8 Chequer Street, St Albans, Hertfordshire AL1 3XZ; 0727 67333

National Out of School Alliance Ltd (NOOSA)
Oxford House, Derbyshire Street, Bethnal Green Road, London E2 6HG; 01-739 4787

National Register of Warranted Builders
Telephone 01-242 7583

National Society for the Prevention of Cruelty to Children (NSPCC)
67 Saffron Hill, London EC1N 8RF; 01-242 1626

The National Toy Libraries Association *see* Playmatters

National Youth Bureau
17–23 Albion Street, Leicester LE1 6GD

Nottingham Educational Supplies (NES)
Ludlow Hill Road, West Bridgford, Nottingham NG2 6HD; 0602 234251

Offspring
E J Arnold & Sons Ltd, Butterfly Street, Leeds LS10 3TS

The Open University
Walton Hall, Milton Keynes, Buckinghamshire MK7 6AA; 0908 74066

Oxford Creche Development Project
St Michael's School, Marston Road, Oxford OX3 0EJ; 0865 251935

Parents Advice Line
PO Box 161, Rode, Bath, Avon BA3 6YD; 0898 333002

Philip & Tacey Ltd
North Way, Andover, Hampshire SP10 5BA; 0264 332171

Playgear Ltd
3 Dennis Parade, Winchmore Hill Road, London N14; 01-882 1293

Playmatters/The National Toy Libraries Association
68 Churchway, London NW1 1LT; 01-387 9592

Playmobil (UK) Ltd
34 Orchard Street, Swansea SA1 5AU; 0792 465559

Polydron UK Ltd
Unit 12, Staveley Way, Brixworth Industrial Estate, Brixworth, Northamptonshire NN6 9EU; 0604 881176

Pre-school Playgroups Association (PPA)
PPA National Centre, 61-63 King's Cross Road, London WC1X 9LL; 01-833 0991

Eastern: First Floor, 4a Gonville Place, Cambridge CB1 1LY; 0223 311908

East Midlands: Willson House, 25-29 Derby Road, Nottingham NG1 5AW; 0602 475906

Greater London: 314-316 Vauxhall Bridge Road, London SW1V 1AA; 01-828 2417

Northern: MEA House, 2nd Floor, Ellison Place, Newcastle upon Tyne NE1 8XS; 091-232 0361

North West: Hotspur House, Gloucester Street, Manchester M1 5QR; 061-236 7847

South East: Neale House, Moat Road, East Grinstead, West Sussex RH19 3LB; 0342 312553

Southern: St Mary's Centre, Chain Street, Reading, Berkshire RG1 2HX; 0734 594064

South West: Room 15, 236 High Street, Exeter EX4 3NN; 0392 58623

West Midlands: Third Floor, Piccadilly Arcade, New Street, Birmingham B2 4HD; 021-643 0063

Yorkshire and Humberside: Fourth Floor, Centenary House, North Street, Leeds LS2 8AY; 0532 452514

Irish Pre-school Playgroups Association (SIPPA)
19 Wicklow Street, Dublin 2; 0001 719245

Northern Ireland Pre-school Playgroups Association (NIPPA)
11 Wellington Park, Belfast BT9 6DJ; 0232 662825

Pre-school Playgroups Association (PPA) Promotion
The Hill School Terrapin, Peppard Road, Caversham, Reading, Berkshire RG4 8TU; 0734 476755

The Prince's Youth Business Trust
8 Jockeys Fields, London WC1R 4TJ; 01-430 0521

Professional Association of Nursery Nurses (PANN)
99 Friar Gate, Derby DE1 1EZ; 0332 43029

Project Fullemploy
102 Park Village East, London NW1 3SP; 01-387 1222

Ravensburger (Fisher Price)
Monks Mead House, Bath Road, Hare Hatch, Reading, Berkshire RG10 9SA; 073522 4481

The Registrar of Companies *see also* Companies Registration Office
Companies House, 55 City Road, London EC1Y 1BB; 01-253 9393

Royal Institution of Chartered Surveyors
12 Great George Street, Parliament Square, London SW1P 3AD; 01-222 7000

Royal Society for Mentally Handicapped Children (MENCAP)
National Centre, 123 Golden Lane, London EC1Y 0RT; 01-253 9433

Royal Society for Prevention of Accidents (RoSPA)
Safety Education Department, Cannon House, The Priory, Queensway, Birmingham B4 6BS; 021-200 2461

Rural Development Commission
11 Cowley Street, London SW1P 3NA; 01-276 6969

St John Ambulance Brigade and Association
National and Overseas Headquarters, 1 Grosvenor Crescent, London SW1X 7EE; 01-235 5231; *see also* St John Ambulance in your local telephone book

St Nicholas Training Centre for the Montessori Method of Education/St Nicholas Montessori College
23–24 Prince's Gate, London SW7 1PT; 01-225 1277

The School of Modern Montessori
Department 2, PO Box 51, London E11 1TD; 01-539 0160

Scottish Business in the Community
Romano House, 43 Station Road, Corstorphine, Edinburgh EH12 7AF; 031-334 9876

Scottish Community Education Council
Atholl House, 2 Canning Street, Edinburgh EH3 8EG; 031-229 2433

Scottish Development Agency
Small Business Division, Rosebery House, Haymarket Terrace, Edinburgh EH12 5EZ; 031-337 9595

Scottish Nursery Nurses' Board (SNNB)
6 Kilnford Crescent, Dundonald, Kilmarnock, Ayrshire KA2 9DW; 0563 850057

Scottish Pre-school Playgroups Association (SPPA)
16 Sandyford Place, Glasgow G3 7NB

Scottish Vocational Education Council (SCOTVEC)
Hanover House, 24 Douglas Street, Glasgow G2 7NQ; 041-248 7900

The Small Business Bureau
32 Smith Square, London SW1P 3HH; 01-222 9000

Small Firms Centres
Ring the operator on 100 and ask for Freefone Enterprise. You will be put in touch with your nearest centre.

The Sports Council
16 Upper Woburn Place, London WC1H 0QP; 01-388 1277

The Standing Conference of Principals
Edge Hill College of Higher Education, Ormskirk, Lancashire L39 4QP; 0695 75171

Tomy UK Ltd
Wells House, 231 High Street, Sutton, Surrey SM1 1LD; 01-661 1547

Toys Direct
Poplar Hill, Elmsett, Ipswich, Suffolk 1P7 6LN; 0473 824116

The Training Agency
Moorfoot, Sheffield S1 4PQ; 0742 753275 and regional offices

Tumble Tots (UK) Ltd
Cousin Lane, London EC4R 3TE; 01-621 0904

Under-Fives Unit
National Children's Bureau, 8 Wakley Street, London EC1V 7QE; 01-278 9441

The Volunteer Centre
29 Lower King's Road, Berkhamsted, Hertfordshire HP4 7BA; 0442 873311

Volunteers Advisory Service
London Voluntary Service Council, 68 Charlton Street, London NW1 1JR; 01-388 0241

Waddingtons Games Ltd
Castle Gate, Oulton, Leeds, Yorkshire LS26 8HG; 0532 82105

Wages Inspectorate
Head Office: Stead House, 11 Tothill Street, London SW1H 9NF; 01-273 4812

Wales Council for Voluntary Action
Llys Ifor, Crescent Road, Caerphilly, Mid Glamorgan CF5 1XL

Wales Pre-school Playgroups Association
2A Chester Street, Wrexham, Clwyd LL13 8BD; 0978 358195

Welsh Development Agency
Head Office: Treforest Industrial Estate, Pontypridd, Mid Glamorgan CF37 5UT; 044 384 1666

Workplace Nurseries Ltd
77 Holloway Road, London N7 8JZ; 01-700 0281

Wyeth Laboratories
Huntercombe Lane South, Taplow, Maidenhead, Berkshire SL6 OPH; 0628 604377

Chapter 15

Further Reading

The Good Toy Guide from Playmatters/The National Toy Libraries Association.

How to Buy a Business: The Daily Telegraph Guide, 2nd edition, P Farrell, 1989, from Kogan Page.

How to Choose Business Premises: A Guide for the Small Firm, H Green, B Chalkley and P Foley, 1986, from Kogan Page.

Information Pack on the Under-Fives from Under-Fives Unit.

Nursery World, every alternate Thursday, from newsagents if ordered.

Play and Things to Play With from the Health Education Authority.

Playgroup and Nurseries Newsletter, bi-monthly from Microfount, 14 Boltons Court, 216-222 Old Brompton Road, London SW5 0BZ. Annual subscription £10 (1989/90).

Pre-school Playgroups: A Handbook, J Lucas and A Henderson, from Allen & Unwin.

Pre-school Playgroups Association (PPA) Publications from PPA Promotion.

Raising Finance: The Guardian Guide for the Small Business, 3rd edition, C Woodcock, 1989, from Kogan Page.

The Small Business Guide, C Barrow, from BBC Publications.

Starting a Successful Small Business, 2nd edition, M J Morris, 1989, from Kogan Page.

Successful Marketing for the Small Business: The Daily Telegraph Guide, 2nd edition, D Patten, 1989, from Kogan Page.

Working for Yourself: The Daily Telegraph Guide to Self-Employment, 10th edition, G Golzen, 1988, from Kogan Page.

Index

Accident book 64, 89
report to local authority 89
Accidents 87-9, 90
household chemicals 87-8
Accountant 28, 103-4
Accounts 10, 64, 99-130, 135-8
Accumulated surplus *see* Profit
Administration 63
Adult and toddler group 13
Advertising 51, 53
a post 33-4
Agreement between parent and childminder 132, 133-6
AIDS 89-90, 138
Allergies 64
Analysis columns 106-9, 113
Analysis tables 101-2
Annual accounts 111-15
Annual return 104
Annual turnover 114, 130
Apples Nursery School 49, 151-3
Arts and crafts projects 91-2
Association of British Insurers 68, 70, 72, 74, 158
Auditor 111

Baby seat 131
Balance sheet 111-12
Balanced diet 82-3
vitamins 82-3
Bank account 20-21, 102-3
interest and charges 100, 115-17
paying-in book 100, 103, 110, 115, 129
Bank manager 28, 103
Bank mandate 103
Bank reconciliation statement 116-17
Bank statement 100, 102, 103, 115-17
abbreviations 115
interest to date 115
Billing parents 46, 117-18
Blue Arrow Personnel Services 10, 159
Bookkeeper 104
Books 95-6
Break-even point 20, 153, 156
Bridgewater Square Nursery 155-7
British Insurance Brokers' Association 68-9, 159
British Standards Institution 85-6, 159
BTEC 159
first courses 149
National Diploma in Caring Services (Nursery Nursing) 31, 33, 141, 143-4
training for small firms 148-9
Budget update 123
Building and repairs 109, 111-14
Buildings insurance 72
Business courses 148
Business Expansion Scheme (BES) 22, 160
Business identity 18, 25, 112
Business in the Community 23, 160
Business plan 19, 22
Buying a playgroup or nursery 28

Camp, playscheme, franchise 16-17
Carer and toddler group 13
Cash book 100-101, 103-4, 107, 109-11, 112-13, 115-17, 119, 129
bank pages 109
payments section 112-13
receipts section 110
Cash-flow forecast 19-20
Certificate of Education in Nursery/Infant Teaching 140, 148; *see also* Teacher
Certificate of incorporation 102
Chartered accountant 112
Chartered surveyor 28
Cheque book 100, 129
stubs 100, 119
paid cheques 103
Cheques issued book 119
Cheque serial number 106, 119
Child abuse 89
Child Accident Prevention Trust 131, 160

Child care courses 139, 140-49
Child care organisations 76-9
Child care qualifications 31-3
  see also specific qualifications
Child care voucher scheme 10
Childminder 11-13, 30, 38, 131-9
  child to minder ratio 30, 131
  competition 138
  hourly rate 133, 135
  low income families 136
  prospects and support 138-9
Children's Legal Centre 136, 160
Child's record card 135; *see also* Registration form
Child to helper ratio 29-31, 115
Chiltern Nursery Training College 145
  Child Care Certificate 32, 144-5
Citizens' Advice Bureau 136
Clothing allowance 43
Coding claim P15 122, 124
Collector of Taxes 112, 126-7
  PAYE audit 129
  registration with 123
College of higher education 33, 140-44
Colours, numbers, letters 96
Community Education Development Centre (CEDC) 139, 160
Community Playthings 55, 160
Companies Act 1981 27
Composite pictures 93
Computerised payroll 129
Computers 97
Consumables 60-61, 100, 109, 111-14
Contingency liability 71
Contract 38-41
Cooking 93, 133
Cooperative 25, 102, 130
CORGI 85, 161
Corporation tax 25, 130
Correspondence courses 148
Cot safety 85-6
Creche 9, 10, 12, 46, 48, 51, 64, 99, 125, 129
  child to helper ratio 30
  definition 15-16
  one-off 63
Cromwell Creche 150-51

Day care group 15
Day nursery 9, 12, 48, 51, 64, 69, 99, 125, 129
  child to helper ratio 30
  definition 15
Deductions working sheet P11 100, 122-4, 127-9
Deficit *see* Loss
Delivery notice 119
Direct debit 69, 116
Doing the books 103-4
Drawing and painting 92

Early Learning Centre 55-6, 94, 98, 161
Eating together 95
Electricity and gas supply 85
Emergency code 124; *see also* Income tax
Employee's annual statement, declaration and certificate 120, 128
Employer's liability 70
  certificate of 70
Employer's Stationery Order Form 122
Employment Act *1972* 39, 41
Employment Protection Act *1975* 39, 41-2
End of financial year 108, 111-12, 128, 137
End of year return P14 120, 128
Enterprise Allowance Scheme 22, 162
Enterprise Zone 23
Equal Opportunities Commission 38, 162
Equipment 10, 55-63, 100, 108-9, 111, 112-14, 131
  faulty goods 62
  insurance 70-71
  mail order 55
  receipt of goods 61
Extended day playgroup 13

Family Credit 132, 138
Federation of Master Builders 27, 162
Fee account 117-18
Fees 45, 48, 51, 99, 101-2, 110, 114-15, 135-6, 138
FIMBRA 68, 162
Finance 10, 18-23, 103
  bank loan 20, 25
  building society mortgage 20
  collateral 18
  government schemes 22-3
  grants 21-2
  interest rates 20-21
Fire regulations 27
First aid box 86

contents 87
First aid courses 87
Food additives and E numbers 83-4
Food Labelling Regulations 83
Food and drink 63-5
Food storage and cooking 83
Free pay to date 126-7
Freezer insurance 65, 71
Fund raising 66-7, 99, 114

Galt 55, 67, 162
Games 95
Getting and keeping helpers 10, 29-44
Gingerbread 16, 79, 135, 162
Gross pay to date 41, 126-7

Health and safety 80-90, 131
Health and Safety at Work Act *1974* 40-42
Health visitor 131-2
Helper 10, 29-44, 80, 115, 120-22, 128
courses 140-49
daily duties 36, 42, 63
definition 10
dismissal 39
legislation 39, 41-2
selection 33-5
supervision 42
volunteers 34
HIV-positive children *see* AIDS
HM Inspector of Taxes 123-4, 128; *see also* Collector of Taxes

Immunisation 80
Imprest 106; *see also* Petty cash
Income and expenditure account 103-4, 111-15, 129-30, 138
Income Support 132, 138
Income tax 100, 104, 109, 124-7; *see also* Tax
basic rate 125, 129
emergency code 123-4
payment of 123, 126
threshold 119, 122-5, 129
Independent Schools Information Service (ISIS) Under-Fives Sheet 51, 163
Infectious diseases 80-81
Inland Revenue 43, 68, 102, 128-9, 137
deductible expense 21, 68, 136; *see also* Payments
Inland Revenue New Employers Starter Pack 102, 119-23, 128
Insurance 10, 68-79, 109, 114, 133
crime reference number 74
how to make a claim 74
premiums 69-70, 111-13, 133
proposal form 69, 71
PPA group insurance 69
International Correspondence Schools (ICS) 148, 163
Interviews 150-57
Inventory of equipment 63, 75-6, 129
Invoices 103, 105, 129
filing 103-4, 110, 119
paying 119

Jigsaw puzzles etc 94
Jobcentre 22, 34
Job description 35-6
Joint and severally guaranteed loan 21, 25, 103

Key person insurance 73

Law Society 28, 164
Leaflet and brochure 45-6, 48-51, 53
Lessons or play 91-8
Letterhead 45-6
Letter of employment *see* Contract
Letter offering employment 37
Limited liability 25
Loaned books, toys and tapes 61
Loan Guarantee Scheme 22
Local authority lists 50
Local enterprise agencies 23
Local press 47
Logo 45-6
London Food Commission 84, 164
London Montessori Centre 32, 146, 164
NNEB qualifications 31, 147
Nursery Foundation Teaching Diploma 31, 146
Lone parent allowance 138
Loos 27
Loss 115
Loss of income 72
Loss of money insurance 71-2

M1(W1) 125-8
MA1 121
Mat B1 120-21
Maps, ethnic groups 97
Married man's allowance 125
Memorandum and Articles of Association 102

Memory, odd one out 96-7
Milk refund 64-5, 99, 115, 137
  WF/DN 15, 65, 137
  WF/DN16A 65-6
MMR immunisation 80
Montessori Association of Teachers and Schools (MATS) 78-9, 165
  membership 78-9
Montessori Equipment Company 15, 55, 79, 165
Montessori Method 15, 55, 141
Montessori nursery school 31, 79, 140
  definition 15
Montessori teacher 10, 15, 79, 139, 147
Montessori workshops 79, 147

NALGO 16, 165
Name 18, 26-7
Nanny 10, 13, 32; *see also* Nursery nurse (NNEB)
National Association of Certificated Nursery Nurses (NACNN) 35, 165
National Childminding Association 79, 89, 133-5, 138-9, 165
  membership 133
National Children's Bureau 79, 165
National Insurance contributions 100, 104, 109, 114, 120
  payment of 123, 126
  threshold 119-21, 123-5, 129, 138
National Insurance number 120, 123-4, 128
National Nursery Examination Board (NNEB) 31-3, 35, 141-2, 144-5, 147, 166
National Out of School Alliance (NOOSA) 16, 166
Net pay 41, 127
Norland Diploma and Badge 32, 145
Norland Nursery Training College 144
Norland Preliminary Certificate 32
Nottingham Educational Supplies (NES) 55, 62-3, 166
NSPCC 89, 166
Nurseries and Childminders Regulation Act *1948* as amended by the Health Services and Public Health Act *1968* 26, 38, 74, 100, 132
Nursery nurse 10, 30-31, 35, 37, 141-3
Nursery school 9, 11-12, 91, 97, 122, 125, 140
  child to helper ratio 30
  definition 14, 30
  lessons or play 91-8

Occupational pension scheme 128
Open days, fêtes, bazaars 53-4, 67
Open University 139, 166
  courses 148
Order book 101-2, 119
Outdoor activities 95
Outdoor facilities 27
Overheads 19, 100, 136
Oxford Creche Development Project 16, 141, 166

P45 122-4, 128-9
  tax code 123
P46 122-4, 129
P60 *see* End of year return P14
Parent and toddler group, definition 13
Partnership 21, 25, 102, 104, 130
PAYE *see* Income tax
Payments 19, 99-100, 103, 107-9, 111-16
Payslip booklet P30BC(Z) 123, 129
Period of notice 118
Personal accident 72
Personal insurance 73
Petty cash 104-9, 114
  bags 104-5
  book 100-105, 108, 115, 129
  box 102, 104, 106
  breakdown 108-9, 129
  entries in book 106-7
  float 104, 106-7, 109
  imprest 106
  voucher 101-2, 105-6, 129
Philip & Tacey 55, 166
Planning permission 27-8
Playdough 60, 93
Playgroup 9, 11-12, 69, 90, 115, 122, 125, 129, 139, 141
  child to helper ratio 29-30
  definition 12-13
Playgroup leader 10, 32-3, 35, 120-21
Playhouse and imaginary play 93
Playmatters/The National Toy Libraries Association 14, 55-6, 79, 166
Polio vaccine 80

Pooh Corner Montessori Nursery School 153-4
PPA 9, 13, 17, 35, 38-41, 42, 55-6, 63, 67, 76, 87-9, 91, 101, 109, 111, 115, 133, 139, 167
  Bonus Scheme 56, 77
  courses 32-3, 91, 140-41, 146
  insurance 78
  membership 77
  Sample contract of employment 38-40
  Sample tenancy agreement 38
Premises 10, 12, 17-18, 20, 23-5, 27, 51
  change of 73-4
Pre-school adviser 26, 132, 137-8
Pre-school Playgroups Association 167; *see also* PPA
Press release 45-7
Princess Christian College 144, 158
  Certificate 32, 145
Prince's Youth Business Trust 22, 167
Printing 92
Private limited company 25, 102-3, 111-12, 130
Professional Association of Nursery Nurses (PANN) 35, 43-4, 79, 167
Profit 114-15, 130, 137-8
Profit and loss account 20
Profit-sharing scheme 115
Promotion and advertising 10, 45-54, 131
  t-shirts and sweatshirts 66
Public liability 70

Reaction to milk, eggs, wheat, fish 82
Read and write 97-8
  workbooks 98
Recommendations 53
Receipts 19, 99, 100, 103, 107-9, 112-16
Redundancy Payments Act *1965* 40-41
Register 101, 129, 138
Registered General Nurse (RGN) 32, 35, 148
Registered Sick Children's Nurse (RSCN) 32, 148
Registrar of Companies 111, 160, 168
Registration form 51-2, 64, 80, 82, 88
Registration with Social Services Department of local authority
  child 135
  childminder 130-33
  helper 38, 132
  nursery 10-11, 17-18, 26, 30-31, 140
  playgroup 10-11, 17-18, 26, 30-31, 140
Rent 109, 111-13
Returned cheques 117
Road safety 86
Royal Society for Prevention of Accidents (RoSPA) 86-9, 168
Royal Society of Health Diploma of Nursery Nursing 32, 145
Rural Development Commission 21, 168

SMP.1 121
SSPI(E) 121
SSPI(T) 121
St John Ambulance 87, 168
  Adult First Aid Certificate 87
St Nicholas Montessori College 32, 147, 168
  Diploma 31, 147
Salaries 42-4, 64, 99, 104, 109, 114, 119-28
Science 97
Scottish Business in the Community 23, 168
Scottish Nursery Nurses' Board (SNNB) 142-3, 168
Scottish Vocational Education Council (SCOTVEC) 143, 168
Section 53 Determination letter 27
Sewing and threading 94
Signatories 103
Signboard 27, 53
Singing and music 94
Single person's allowance 125, 138
Small Firms Centre 23, 169
Small Firms Service 23
Smocks 57, 62-3, 92
Social Services Department 10-11, 17-18, 26, 30-31, 38, 80, 99, 101, 131-41
  help for low income families 136
Sole trader 25, 102-4, 130
Solicitor 28
Sports Council 21, 169
Stairs 86
Standing order 116
Stationery clip 102, 105
Stationery for keeping accounts 101-2
Statutory group 9, 31

Statutory maternity pay (SMP) 42, 120-21, 129
  exemptions 120
  forms 121
  rates 120-21
Statutory sick pay (SSP) 121, 129
  rates 121

Tax
  code 123, 126, 128
  inspector 111
  office 124, 126, 129
  office reference number 124, 128
  refund 126
  relief 21-2
  tables 119, 123, 126
Taxable pay to date 126-7
Teacher 10, 14, 30, 32, 35, 140
Telling the time 96
Till receipt 105
Toy library 14
Toys, puppets, mobiles 93
Training Agency 21, 169
Triple injection 80
Tumble Tots 16-17, 169
Types of child care 11-17
  full-time care 17
  part-time care 17

Under-fives group 13
Under-Fives Unit 169; *see also* National Children's Bureau

VAT 74, 100, 105
Voluntary group 9, 31, 102

Wages slip 101-2, 127, 129
Waiting list 18
Weighing and measuring 94
Windows and doors 84-5
Workplace nurseries 16, 79, 169
Workplace nursery 9-10, 12, 46, 48, 99, 125
  child to helper ratio 30
  credit insurance 73
  definition 16
Written receipt 105

Yellow Pages 50-51, 53, 55
Youth Training Scheme (YTS) 79, 144